Games and Spor

Activity in the Primary School

General Editor: Don Buckland

Games and Sports

by

W. M. Wise

Senior Lecturer in Physical Education
Brighton College of Education

Heinemann Educational Books
London

Heinemann Educational Books Ltd
22 Bedford Square, London WC1B 3HH

LONDON EDINBURGH MELBOURNE AUCKLAND
HONG KONG SINGAPORE KUALA LUMPUR NEW DELHI
IBADAN NAIROBI JOHANNESBURG
EXETER (NH) KINGSTON PORT OF SPAIN

ISBN 0 435 80603 3

Set, printed and bound in Great Britain by
Fakenham Press Limited, Fakenham, Norfolk

Contents

Introduction to the Series

Young children have an instinctive delight in movement. They respond with pleasure to a natural urge to run, jump, throw, climb and dance. The teacher who sets out to develop this energy into useful and creative activities can expect his pupils to be enthusiastic and responsive. The experience is likely to be particularly rewarding for both teacher and class, for during the period of development covered by this series of handbooks, the growth of skill, awareness, versatility and confidence is dramatic. The teacher does not need to be an expert performer or to hold specialist qualifications in physical education. In fact, one hopes that the children in our Infant and Junior Schools will continue to be taught by those who are first and foremost experts in the teaching of children. In Middle Schools a qualified teacher who can serve as the power house for physical education will be needed, although it is to be hoped that he will not adopt the traditional role of the specialist. His task will be to inspire, enthuse, co-ordinate and guide the rest of the staff in their work with their classes, and, by virtue of his own personal ability and example, to set the tempo of the extra-curricular programme.

Moving and Growing drew attention to the ways in which children learn – by repetition, by exploration, through creation, through contact with each other, with the teacher and other adults. The teacher will create learning situations according to the nature of each individual child and the stage he has reached. Planning, organization and knowledge are necessary, and this series of handbooks sets out to provide this help. They offer suggestions for work in a balanced programme of physical education for the stages of education suggested by the Plowden Report, i.e. the first eight years of compulsory schooling from five years to twelve plus.

Drama is included in the series, in addition to Games, Gymnastics, Swimming and Dance, because of its obvious links with movement, and its value as an activity whereby so much of the work in the Primary

School may be integrated. It is not suggested that all five aspects of physical education will be covered concurrently. It might be more effective to deal intensively with one or two activities for a concentrated block of time. We do suggest, however, that all aspects should be included in a balanced programme for each stage of primary education.

The tremendous growth of new subjects and new approaches in the Primary School in recent years has made very great demands upon the teacher. Time for planning and preparation is precious, and there is a danger that physical education will either be seen merely as a chance for letting off steam, or will be squeezed out altogether by the pressure of other work. It is hoped that this series will enable the teacher to see the subject as contributing to the process of education as a whole; as another way of assisting the development of people.

January, 1969.   DON BUCKLAND
                                            General Editor

Acknowledgements

The material contained within this book has been assembled from a variety of sources with a view to presenting a composite body of information covering the whole area of Games and Sports in one volume. Much of the source material has been amended to suit the approaches recommended, nevertheless grateful acknowledgement is made to the following sources of information.

1. 1933 Syllabus, H.M.S.O.
2. *Planning the Programme*, H.M.S.O.
3. *Small Side Team Games*, Army Sports Control Board.
4. *Introduction to Netball in Junior Schools*, All England Netball Association.
5. *Hockey in the Primary School* All England Womens Hockey Association.
6. *Activity Games*, P. M. Kingston.
7. *Games Worth Playing*, D. McCuaig and G. S. Clark.

8. *Coaching Rugby Footballers*, R.F.U.
9. 'Introduction to Junior Basketball', article by B. Coleman.
10. *Some aspects of the Law relating to P. E. Teachers*, P. E. Association of G.B.
11. *Safety at School*, Education Pamphlet No. 53, H.M.S.O.
12. *Primary School P.E.*, C. Meek
13. *Know the Game: Batinton* and conversations with P. Hanna.
14. *Padder Tennis*, Slazengers.
15. *Primary Soccer*, pamphlet produced by author with the able and experienced assistance of Mr P. R. Walters, Mr D. G. King, Mr R Clark, Mr P. Bates and Mr D. Pritchard for the Bridgwater Primary Schools Sports Association.

My grateful thanks also to my colleagues in Somerset for their conscious and unconscious assistance by thought, word and deed, and to the numerous teachers from all kinds of schools whose genuine concern for the less able skill learner may yet drastically alter the teaching of games at their root source.

Cover photographs taken at Woodingdean County Primary School (J.M. and I.), Brighton, by kind permission of the Headmaster, Mr N. J. M. Hagard. Photographer: Mr S. R. Jennings, A.T.C., Brighton College of Education.

Chapter 1: Introduction

Games and sports – the continuing heritage of the British child. Such activities are part of our social structure, accepted and encouraged by parents, the instinctive delight of most young children and within the living experience of all teachers.

The teaching of such activities needs thought and organization in order that the material and situations presented may offer a measure of success and encouragement to ALL abilities in the varying age-ranges taking part. Building on the natural urge of the infant to run, throw, skip and hop, a pattern of work develops which may well involve the early maturers in our national team games, but for the majority of top juniors, will culminate in scaled down versions more suited to their abilities at that time.

Social conditions are such that many children experience their only opportunity to learn a variety of physical skills, and release their natural energy in this sphere at school. With both parents working, television, cars, bingo, overtime and flat-living, it is essential that the time allocated should be used to the full. The 'longer playtime', or 'if you don't behave there will be no games' approaches still occur and are a plain avoidance of duty. Play tends to be spontaneous, satisfying and absorbing, lacking any overall end. Whilst these elements should be fostered in games and sports, these activities require deliberation and thought on both teachers' and pupils' part to direct them towards the main stream of educational endeavour. Young children enjoy and NEED the physical release afforded by such activities, and one has only to observe the energy and enthusiasm displayed in a well organized and controlled lesson to be convinced of its value educationally.

Some teachers may naturally be concerned that they feel incapable of demonstrating the necessary skills. Although this worry is understandable, it should not prove too great an obstacle since the real essentials successfully to teach physical activities in this age-range are controlled enthusiasm, planning, good humour, the philosophy of encouraging and involving ALL the children, and a personal stoicism concerning the weather. A vigorous controlled burst of outdoor activity in a long school day benefits both teacher and pupil even in inclement conditions.

Teaching Principles

The essential principles to be borne in mind when planning and teaching games and sports are identical with those applied to other aspects of the young child's education, namely:

1. Enjoyment linked with maximum activity for all participants.
2. Presentation of attainable objectives commensurate with age and ability.
3. Variety of skill opportunities.
4. Wherever possible, encouragement by incidental coaching.
5. Emphasis on learning by doing – with the essential minimum of explanation.
6. Realization that many repetitions are necessary for most children to increase their level of skill.

Overall Guide Lines

Infants: free skill practices using large balls, small balls, bats, sticks, bean bags, hoops, and shuttles as individuals, guided play through indirect approach with counting repetitions strongly in evidence. A foundation course should be aimed at improving the level and variety of skills in the most enjoyable and incidental manner possible. In many cases the atmosphere created by the teacher allows the nervous and timid child to practise, slowly to gain confidence, shielded from more boisterous playmates who may also benefit from more purposeful direction of their energies.

Lower Juniors: for some, free skill practices should be continued, but for the majority a gradual change towards social activities; co-operation with a partner in kicking and hitting activities strongly emphasizing the CO-OPERATION aspect in the early stages. Although elements of competition may appear very quickly, the stress towards co-operation at this stage will enable more skills to be acquired to supplement more skilful competition later. More direct teaching methods mixed with longer periods of practice will often be found to be the best teaching technique for children of this age. The ablest players will often introduce competitive elements, and towards the end of this time a combination of co-operation and friendly competition is desirable.

Juniors: approached in the right way this is the great age for acquiring skills and attitudes favourable to physical activity which may have effects of tremendous personal and national consequence. If, however, the criteria of the school is solely the successful team in its full tactical, physical and social implications, there is a real danger that, particularly in large schools, this ideal age for learning physical skills will be squandered by concentration on the select. Whilst respecting the tremendous service many teachers have given (and indeed continue to give) to the organization of school leagues, and recognizing that physically mature and naturally able children are in certain measure capable of these standards, there is no doubt that over emphasis on the few serves only to discourage the many. Without wishing to deprive the ablest of the physical endeavour and competition which they require, the greatest demand for ALL the children is organized teaching of skills to be used in small side or scaled down versions of major games. First acquaintances with physical experiences are critical to both learning and continuance, and it is possible at this stage to mar a child's attitude, if he instinctively knows that the step ahead is too great. Emphasis therefore should be towards direct teaching of essential aspects of major games, linked in the same lesson with the opportunity to try these slowly maturing skills in small side versions of the particular game with the minimum of rules.

This overall pattern has been used for many years with great human understanding by many Primary teachers. Recent developments of multi-purpose apparatus has brought a variety of small-side games within the scope of the Junior school. Together with a more child-centred philosophy, these have enabled positive goals to be included in an overall plan in a wide variety of interesting and purposeful activities in addition to the accepted major games.

The aim therefore should be to lay a broad foundation of slowly developing games skills which, together with experiences of dance, dance-drama, gymnastics and swimming, will enable the great majority of children confidently to approach new physical experiences awaiting them as they mature. In order that they may fully benefit, it follows that the majority of these activities, at more structured and competitive levels commensurate with maturational and interest changes, should appear within the curriculum, or as club activities in Middle or Secondary schools. Realistically 'guided choice' may have to operate because of limitations of numbers, facilities and staffing. The wider programme has been the major feature of change in many Secondary schools in the past decade; if therefore the children entering this stage of their educational road had already had some experience of the possible variety of activities, it would encourage those whose interest in the nationally accepted games had rarely existed or waned to seek a new outlet with much more confidence. The proposed creation of Middle schools in some areas may well be crucial in bridging the physical gap, particularly if the schools are staffed by non-specialist teachers of physical activities. The opportunity to continue the kind of overall plan envisaged here through the rather more difficult and often slightly less enthusiastic maturational years may well be lost if such schools lose sight of the 'many' at the age at which they would previously have transferred to a Secondary school.

Chapter 2: Infants

The establishment of habits of order and self-control in the children cannot be too highly stressed, and it is recommended that teachers should firmly control all necessary pre-lesson preparation, gradually allowing more freedom as and when the children are able to use it sensibly. Thorough preparation of lessons, organization of equipment, and preliminary training in changing, handling apparatus, and attention are essential if real progress is to be achieved.

As the class become more proficient at the following:
- (a) changing quickly and quietly
- (b) keeping apparatus still during explanations
- (c) finding individual spaces in which to work
- (d) going to group places without fuss and with certainty
- (e) working individually without hindering others
- (f) using common sense

the teacher's role will be direct with the object of creating an ordered society in which real experimentation can take place.

Apparatus

Since it is rarely possible to provide each class with its own set of small apparatus, co-operation between all teachers in a school is vital.

At this stage many activities are best introduced as class activities with each child using the same piece of equipment in a variety of ways. A wheeled storage trolley carrying light wire containers for smaller items, with specially designed spaces for canes, skittles, and hoops greatly assists both storage and transportation. Four larger containers, e.g. wicker baskets, can be used to store and transport all the larger equipment such as 4-in. and 7-in. playballs.

Much time will be saved, efficiency achieved, and nerves less frayed if children are thoroughly trained from the start to return apparatus to its proper place, so that it is ready and easily available for use by the next class. It is not the teacher's job to get out or issue equipment. With quiet persistence the children can soon be trained to have the required apparatus ready for the lesson, and to return it neatly and quickly to its store.

Requirements (class of 30)

30 7-in. plastic balls	30 playbats
30 4-in. plastic balls	30 quoits
30 7-oz. Frido balls.	30 bean bags
30 gamester balls	30 shuttles
30 8-ft skipping ropes	12 canes
30 hoops, various sizes	24 light hoop-holder skittles

Additional items which may prove useful include tennis balls, table tennis balls, and washing-up liquid containers to serve as easy and quiet skittles for aiming practices. Most of these pieces of small equipment will withstand a great deal of use before needing replacement if they are protected from over enthusiastic but possibly misplaced application.

Time Allocation

Indoors: 15–20 minutes per day, possibly linked with Music and Movement to reduce changing time.

Outdoors: a similar allocation of time when the weather allows; after inclement weather or during 'bright spells' slightly longer compensatory periods.

Clothing

Indoors: vest, shorts, or knickers suitable changed footwear.

Outdoors: children are unable to learn when they are cold. Although they must obviously be properly shod in order to run with confidence, there is little point, especially with beginners, in having a hard and fast changing rules for outdoor activities. Commonsense on the teacher's part, based on the acid test of personal changing to brave the elements, often provides a truer guide. However, this test should not lead to the frequent cancellation of the lesson.

Lesson Planning Material
Limbering

Walking ⎫
Running ⎪ emphasis on immediate activity with gradual introduction
Skipping ⎬ of ideas such as stopping and starting, changes of direction,
Hopping ⎪ changes of speed and the encouragement and opportunity of
Jumping ⎭ finding different ways of doing each activity.

Training (as a class)
Activities with Large, Medium and Small Balls, Quoits and Beanbags

1. Free experiment: observation will give a variety of examples which can be demonstrated and attempted.
2. Gradually lead children on to: (*a*) BOUNCING, (*b*) THROWING, (*c*) CATCHING, (*d*) KICKING, (*e*) STOPPING, initially using the playground surface and space around, and eventually rebound surfaces such as walls, and when appropriate, to working in co-operation with a partner.

   All these activities can be indirectly taught by requiring a variety of ways to be practised such as:
   (*a*) on the spot
   (*b*) on the move
   (*c*) using one hand/foot – other hand/foot – both hands
   (*d*) using hands as bats
   (*e*) using the wall to rebound, or as an aiming point
   (*f*) working with a partner
   In this way teachers can shape the lesson and gradually build up both the level and variety of skills in the group.

Counting repetitions, i.e. self-testing of each activity, is often a great incentive to improvement in these early stages particularly if the scores are quickly checked by the teacher.

Activity with Skittles, Canes, Ropes, Hoops

This type of equipment enables indirect but valuable training essential to games and sports such as jumping, landing in various ways and at a variety of speeds, and mental agility related to objects to be pleasantly but directly taught, and greatly assists parts of the later group work.

Children set up pairs of skittles with a cane across each pair spread over the area with hoops lying on the ground in free spaces.

1. Coaching of landing – from any position aiming for light, controlled, easy, relaxed landing bringing the seat down near the heels.
2. Free experiment based on running jumping and landing over canes, in, over and round hoops with encouragement to change direction as often and as quickly as possible, avoiding all obstacles both animate and inanimate.
3. Gradually encourage fewer jumps of better quality by encouraging 'fewer steps and higher jumps', jumps of one foot, jumps off both

feet, use of the arms and body to assist the jump and jumps with turns.
A great deal of active, enjoyable and valuable work related to games
and sports can be introduced in this way.

Activity with Playbats, Shuttles, Gamester and Tennis Balls

1. Free experiment individually with the apparatus, using examples
   selected by observation to encourage further experimentation and
   increase variety.
2. Encouragement to try using different parts of the bat, different body
   positions, and particularly repetitions on the move with self testing
   counting included.
3. Gradual improvement of co-ordination and control, in the air, on
   the ground and against walls, eventually leading to pair work, co-
   operating to see which pair can achieve most successful repetitions.

Group Activities

Organization

1. Groups of four to six children wherever possible.
2. Define working spaces to avoid interference with other groups.
3. Give clear 'challenges' to each group, relating your choice to activities
   previously practised as a class. In smaller group situations more concentrated practice can be achieved and more observation and incidental coaching is often possible.
4. Each group puts out its own apparatus, noting each week at which
   point they should commence the next time. It is rarely practicable
   to achieve any worth-while work if the groups are changed too
   frequently.
5. Order of changing tasks can be introduced either by chalk arrows or
   walking each group to its next area until the pattern is firmly established.
6. One good layout of tasks may well last for a term with minor
   alterations, since in 15-minute lessons only two or three activities
   will be undertaken.
7. Activities chosen should be challenging and purposeful.
8. Use a whistle 'in extremis'.

Ideas for Groups

1. Hoops: bowling for speed, direction and control; in and out of roll-

ing hoop; changing moving hoop with partner travelling in opposite direction; rotating hoop round arm, leg, body.

2. Ropes: how many skips without stopping? – using both feet, one foot, on the spot, on the move – other ways of skipping, skipping with a partner.

3. Skittles and canes: different ways of jumping, gradually increasing height, varying heights of skittles, over and under, group arrange course, ditch jump, two canes supported in parallel gradually increasing gap.

4. Gamester balls: catching, throwing, and particularly aiming either at prepared marks on the wall or at small plastic skittles. Great interest can be added by having a simple scoring system included on the objects.

5. Beanbags: how high can you throw and catch, on the spot, on the move; baskets, graded chalk marks on the ground, aiming – how many can you get in from here?; partners – throwing and catching gradually moving farther away and throwing higher and harder – different parts with which you can catch.

5. Light playbat and shuttlecock: on the spot, how many hits using front/back of the bat, low hits, high hits, mixture of heights, repeat on the move; pairs – co-operation – keep it up and count.

6. Playbat and gamester: same challenges as No. 5 but changing as soon as possible to rebound repetitions with counts against wall and as control gradually grows to rebound co-operation with a partner.

7. 7-in. balls: bouncing and catching on the spot, on the move varying height, speed and direction, moving bounce in and out of simple skittle maze, heading starting by holding ball in both hands and pushing it away with forehead gradually throwing and heading. Ways of throwing and catching in pairs.

8. 7-oz. Frido: kicking preferably from short distance against a wall trying to keep the ball moving with gradually increasing control with emphasis on the use of both feet, kicking at targets, kicking to a partner.

9. Quoits: throwing, catching, rolling and stopping – pairs freely – pairs over suspended rope or cane.

10. 4-in. and smaller balls: strong aiming practice and more exacting dribbling practices.

At later stages groups may be given assorted apparatus with the challenge to 'make up a game'. Such challenges may completely fail, in which case the teacher will give guidance; at other times games will appear to supplement the teacher's store of guidance for future classes. Some combinations of apparatus which lend themselves to this type of choice activities are:

(a) skittles, hoops and beanbags

(b) jumping stands or skittles with rope or canes and large light balls

(c) bats, small ball, skittles

(d) hoops, quoits and 4-in. balls

It is suggested that from these and other ideas which may occur locally due to architectural features, local traditions, or equipment peculiarities, the teacher selects 4, 5 or 6 group activities related to the earlier part of the lesson, decides on suitable challenges and plans the areas in which each is to operate. Having steadfastly inculcated the circulation system the teacher is then free to give indirect coaching encouragement, admonition where necessary, and to observe and draw attention to any particular pieces of work which are noteworthy.

Class Games

The third type of work particularly suitable in these early years is the simple game whose straightforward objectives are high enjoyment, total activity, and low skill element. In the earliest stages the short period available may be completely devoted to this type of companionable and enjoyable activity, but as time passes a gradual change towards the scheme outlined should be noticeable with the occasional class game used either as an introduction where the class all appear at the same time, or preferably at the end of the lesson by curtailing or even at times omitting the group activities.

Certain factors concerned with safety are well considered before embarking on mass activities such as these which involve elements of the chase.

1. Instil the idea of use of space, controlled running and awareness of others, together with the ability to dodge by constant repetition.

2. Behaviour when caught, i.e. to stand still, needs to be taught.

3. Cross slope running.

4. Avoid walls, railings and small spaces as bases.

5. Multiplication of chasers within reason leads to greater activity and better overall spacing.

6. Aim for 'working noise'; other classes may be disturbed, causing personal problems in the near future.

Types of Class Games
Incantations

What is the Time Mr Wolf: whole class or smaller groups in defined areas. Group follows wolf or wolves chanting the title; wolf answers time of choice until he says 'Dinner time'; group races for base, the wolf catching by touch. Change wolves.

Big A Little A: whole class or smaller units in defined spaces. Children advance slowly towards cat or cats who stand with backs to group. Chant Big A (tall as they can), Little A (small as they can), Bouncing B (jump on spot). Cats in the cupboard and can't catch me (advance on toes). Words and actions repeated until someone is near enough to touch the cat. Cat then gives chase catching by touch.

Tom Tiddlers Ground: one or several Tom Tiddlers guard a defined space. The others try to cross this space calling 'I'm on Tom Tiddlers ground.' Once on the space they must try to cross. Those who are caught may either help the catchers or be sent to prison.

Giants and Fairies: two groups. Leader calls 'Fairies' who come out and dance round space. When 'Giants' are called the fairies quickly quit the field leaving the giants to stride and roar in the space. The groups are changed and the game continues.

Mime: children mime movements (and where appropriate and permissible sounds) of objects called out by teacher, e.g. animals, birds, reptiles, cars, aeroplanes.

Chasing Games

All forms of 'Tag' provide a basis of dodging, swerving and other individual avoidance tactics fundamental to contact games. They have a place from time to time in the physical activities of a very wide age-range and may gradually be increased in complexity as ability and sensibility grows.

Some early examples are as follows:

1. *Free Tag:* one or more players are chosen to chase the others – chasers distinguished by braid. When players are touched they may either drop out or join chasers, the game continuing without pause. A

number of short games giving as many as possible the opportunity to be a chaser often ensures maximum activity.

2. *Couple Tag:* chasers in pairs, inside hands joined. When either player touches a runner they become free being replaced by the child touched.

Other forms: start in pairs, add on third person when touched chasing now in a group of three, when a fourth person is touched split group into two couples and continue. Alternatively continue adding children touched to form a 'chain' of chasers.

3. *Free and Caught:* two or more 'chasers', remainder disperse. Immediately a chaser is touched he must stand still but can be released by being touched by a free player. The object of the game is to get everyone standing still, while all the free players try to prevent this happening. Other positions to be adopted when caught may be used, e.g. crouch, sitting.

4. *All-in-tag:* one chaser wearing a braid – anyone touched gets a braid and helps chase the remainder.

5. *Ball Tag:* simplest type is to have two chasers each with light playball who tag runners by throwing ball to hit them preferably below the waist. Complexity can be added if desired by adopting the free and caught rules to the same type of catching procedure.

6. *Keep the Basket Full:* broadcast sowing in all directions by the teacher of small balls, bean bags, playballs (personal choice determined by facilities). Children return the missiles to the basket from which they are immediately re-dispatched in other directions. Encouragement to disperse widely and to watch the flight of the ball will greatly assist both incidental and avoidance learning.

7. *Bean Bag Scramble:* class divided into groups, teacher tosses as many bean bags in the air as possible in all directions. Children catch and collect them each group then counting its score.

8. *Follow the Leader:* small groups each with a leader whom they follow and copy. It is often necessary for the teacher to suggest some possible avenues of thought, e.g. tall, small, quick, slow, directions to prevent constant repetitions of the obvious at a steady speed from being the vogue.

9. *Bogey Ball:* starting from a line, the teacher rolls a big ball forward (one child being ready to field it on the second line). The children try to race the ball before it reaches the line.

10. *All-in-race: scoring runs* – individual running from one line to the other counting their own 'runs', i.e. one for each crossing until stopped. Check scores.
11. *Dancing Feet:* running freely on the signal changing to moving the feet very quickly on the spot – continue.
12. *Dancing on Partner's Head:* sunny day required – one child dodges while his partner tries to dance on the shadow cast by the *head* of the dodger.

Miniature Games

Towards the end of the infant stage a number of activities probably best described as miniature games, which demand concentration but are flexible in the sense of rules, should wherever possible be included. Teachers will obviously choose those most suited to the ability of their children, therefore the following selection should be regarded as an indication of the types of game they might well consider.

Team Circle Dodge Ball

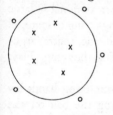

Where possible using a number of small teams. Reds in circle – Blues spaced round outside of circle. Large light ball thrown to hit dodgers below waist or knee – retire when hit.

Can be played to extinction or preferably avoid retirement and record number of hits made by each team in 1, 2, 3 minutes as decided.

Four Court Dodge Ball

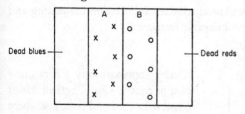

Red team – area 'A'; Blue team – area 'B'. Use 3, 4 or 5 large light balls shared at start equally between both teams.

Ball thrown to hit opponents below knee. When hit, retires behind 'enemy lines' to dead man's ground. From this area continues to attack from the rear. Winning team is the one which completely eliminates opponents from central court.

Bombardment

Several, e.g. 4 or 6 large light balls evenly distributed between teams. Skittles set up in rear of each team – approximately 1 yd apart. Each team sub-divides into attackers and defenders. Defenders prevent balls hitting their skittles in rear and feed ball to their attackers who in turn aim and throw underhand to try to hit their opponents' skittles.

Targets when hit may be left down until a whole set are recumbent or preferably they may be constantly re-set and a score kept over a determined time, e.g. 5 minutes.

Big Side

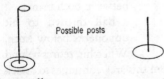

Defined area: goal posts made of bean bags in small piles. Small teams of 4 to 6 mixed.

A. Football: goalkeeper optional – large light playball kicking trying to score.

Rules: NO hands, off-side, centre, arguing, shouting, kissing, hugging. Play, play, play.

B. Handball: same game using hands instead of feet keeping the ball on the ground.

Capable of adaptation in many ways, e.g. basic shinty, hockey will need constant exhortation for passing and spreading out to become noticeable features.

Postball

Circles approximately 5 ft radius – post in centre. Use of netball stands possible in some schools, elsewhere multi-purpose posts in metal sockets advised.

Small teams encourage stopping and passing to unmarked member of one's own team when in possession of the ball. Score by hitting post below goalkeeper's stretch height. Continuous play – ball thrown out by goalkeeper after score. Change keepers during game.

Keep it Up

Rope or net at approximately 4 to 5 ft – higher if ability warrants. Large ball thrown and caught back and forth across net, scoring points when it goes out or hits ground in opponents' court. Encourage great many passes between team-mates each time before ball is returned. Where particularly able groups are concerned encourage fingertip hitting and passing rather than catching.

Bat – Ball – Shuttle – Quoit Games

Any rectangular area either indoors or out can easily be arranged to accommodate a number of simple but enjoyable games using this type of equipment.

A long rope or net (if available) can be stretched along the middle of the length supported at intervals by multi-purpose posts, which serve to indicate court areas, supplemented where possible by chalk or painted lines.

Tennis

Playbats with either gamester or tennis balls – pairs building to fours.
  (*a*) continuous hits co-operating with partner allowing innumerable bounces
  (*b*) continuous hits maximum two bounces
  (*c*) continuous hits one bounce maximum
  (*d*) underhand hit to start – simple game – singles and doubles. This stage may never satisfactorily be reached for those looking for potential champions. Look for enjoyment and slight improvement.
  It is suggested that a net height of 2½ to 3 ft would be suitable. By raising the net height quite arbitrarily according to 'felt-need' the following activities are possible:
  (*a*) use of playbats and inexpensive shuttles, co-operation stressed
  (*b*) use of quoits, pairs building up to small teams

(c) use of large ball, 'keep it up' previously mentioned.

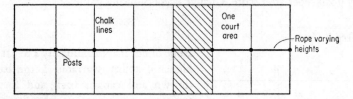

These activities are often more satisfactorily accomplished by children in the Junior school, but many top infants are capable of these skills especially if the teacher herself controls their hitting capacity and perseveres.

Cricket
Five or Six Single Wicket

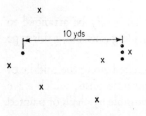

Bat shape preferred to bat. Gamester or tennis ball. Wickets marked on wall, portable wickets if available wicker basket or box (wooden or cardboard).

Rules: underhand bowling from approximately 10 yds; ball to bounce before reaching batsman; each batsman has 6 balls from each player, i.e. if five players and four fielders, he has 24 balls, whether he is out or not; individual scores.

Encourage fair, easy paced bowling, natural hitting, fielding and catching.

French Cricket

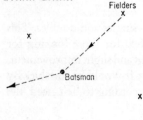

Groups of 4 or 5. Batsman with bat shape protecting legs below knee. Fielders dispersed on all sides one with tennis ball. Tosses ball to try and hit the batsman's legs. Ball is hit or deflected, fielded as soon as possible and bowled from fielder's position. Batsman can either be allowed to turn or obliged to remain continually with feet fixed.

Non-stop Football Cricket

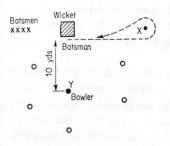

Large wicket, e.g. wicker basket, large box. Large light playball. Teacher or child rolls ball to batsman who kicks it in any direction and immediately departs to run round wicket post or skittle marked 'X'.

Fielders either catch him out, or field ball and return it as quickly as possible to the bowler who keeping his back foot behind point 'Y', bowls whether batsman has returned or not. According to the strength of the kick and efficiency of the fielders the batsman may at his own risk run as many times as he chooses scoring one run for each successful run.

This game may easily be adapted to use of playbat and gamester or tennis ball according to conditions or personal preference.

Dodging Rounders

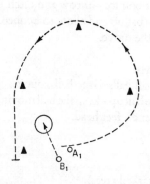

Can be played on a rounders pitch, or on a course marked out by bean bags or skittles either indoors or out, usually with up to 30 players. Large playbats – 4-in. to 7-in. playball. Batting team line up in twos. Fielding side take up positions in the field.

Batsman A1 of the first couple hits the ball and runs round the outside of the course, partner B1 runs to the centre of the circle. Fielders secure the ball and try to hit B1 below waist or knee before the runner completes the course. Teams change when all batting side have had turn of both batting and dodging.

Variations
  1. Whilst A1 runs the course, fielding side have to secure the ball and make four catches between any four separate fielders.
  2. Single runner can be put out either at the base, or hit with ball either in the hand or thrown whilst running round.

The examples of class games quoted are merely indications of the type of games which have been successfully used in Infant schools. Many others exist, and many variations of these are possible. Teachers have their own preferences; ability within classes varies from one area to another and indeed from one year to another, therefore the responsibility of choice of activity is quite rightly the teacher's. Any controlled games activity which provides enjoyment, maximum participation at low skill level will immediately appeal to the majority of the children at this stage.

By the time they move on to the Junior school many will be far more skilful and confident of their own ability to manipulate a variety of games equipment and therefore prepared to progress towards more recognizable games practices and games.

Infants Games Training. Ideas for Teachers
A. How Many?
(Beat your own record – for familiarity and control)
  1. Small balls – bounce and catch – pat bounce – throw and catch.
  2. Bats and balls – bat up – bat down – bat up and allow to bounce.
     (*a*) on spot; (*b*) dancing feet; (*c*) on the move.
  3. Shuttles bat up.
  4. Scoring runs – journeys between lines.
  5. Throw and catch with partner – small balls, large balls, quoits.
  6. Groups of four (large balls) – keep the ball up – keep the ball moving – keep the ball bouncing in circle – hands, feet head.

B. How Far, How High?
  1. High bounce and catch (small ball).
  2. Throwing bean bag for distance (marked areas).
  3. Throwing high – large balls, then small balls, quoits.
  4. Jumping for height – blocks, blocks and canes.
  5. Jumping for distance – (mats) standing, running.
  6. Kicking over lines or ropes.

7. Throwing ball up and hitting over line or ropes.
8. Throwing up and heading large light ball – height and distance.

C. How Close? (for accuracy and skill)
1. Rolling between skittles with partner – small ball, large ball, hoop.
2. Overarm aim at skittle with partner.
3. Underarm aim into basket from given lines – bean bags, small balls, quoits, gamesters.
4. Aiming through horizontal hoop in fours – bean bags, small and large balls.
5. Throwing through vertical hoop in threes – bean bags, small and large balls.
6. Kicking through a goal – pairs one on each side of goal.
7. Individually aiming at wall target, or skittle against wall.

D. Miniature Games
Examples: Cricket in fives, French cricket, Tennis practice at wall, Tennis over rope with partner, Tenniquoit over rope, Catch and Pass Rounders, Rounders Runs, Dodge Ball, Bombardment.

E. Major Points
1. Footwork and keeping on the move.
2. Grips for all hitting actions.
3. Throwing stance allied to catching and fielding positions.
4. Decision on shape of lesson based on ability, space available and equipment.
5. Progression – only the beginning is sheer free play with the apparatus – thence to individual, pair and later group skills emphasizing the measusement of improvement in each situation.
6. Teacher assesses improvement by keeping some record, e.g. jumping.

Chapter 3: Lower Juniors

Lower Junior Stage

The acquisition of games skill does not recognize such arbitrary boundaries as Infants, Lower Juniors, and Upper Juniors. It is a continuing process. There is no sharp divide because the children are chronologically a 'summer holiday' older. Logically therefore many activities previously experienced as infants will be repeated especially in the earliest stages. This repetition of fundamentals need not be protracted but is extremely useful in order to establish a firm base on which the teacher can build in future lessons.

Gradual changes which should occur with the passing of time would be:

(a) more direct coaching of accepted efficient techniques of throwing, jumping, hitting, bowling, catching, kicking and stopping
(b) group situations approximating more closely to parts of games
(c) better standards of performance and longer periods of concentration in class, group and small game time allocations
(d) use of 'active' small size team relays, which present opportunities to build up speed, dodging and ball manipulation on a team competition basis
(e) the encouragement of friendly competition either individually, in pairs or in small groups

General Principles

1. The games period should be fun, stimulating and active, i.e. 'prepared'.
2. Children must be trained to bring out apparatus, and space it so that it can be reached without crowding, and without obstructing useful wall areas.
3. There may be a few minutes of free practice with the apparatus of personal choice singly or in pairs during changing.

4. Apparatus must be returned to the correct place sensibly and checked for both number and condition regularly.
5. Consideration for others in the use of space and apparatus must be instilled if progress is to be achieved.
6. Children must be trained to get into groups quickly, and to play in such groups with the minimum of argument.

Lesson Forms

Form A – Mathematical Progression form preferred by some Teachers

1. Practices singly (*a*) without apparatus, (*b*) with apparatus.
2. Practices in pairs with small ball, bats, sticks, hoops, bean bags.
3. Practices in threes or fours with apparatus.
4. Four, six or eight groups of individuals or partners working with varied apparatus.
5. 'Matches' – 5 or 6 a side with large or small ball and various ways of scoring or with small ball and sticks or bats.

Lessons suitable for both indoors and outdoors can be created to fit this 'form' by selecting one or more practices from each of the following sections allocating the areas most suitable according to individual facilities.

Basic Skills

1. Running at speed.
2. Running with quick dodging.
3. Running changing speed from trotting to sprinting.
4. Throwing underarm and overarm and rolling with small ball.
5. Throwing a large ball with two hands using overhead soccer throw, netball shoulder pass, low underhand pass, chest pass, rugby pass.
6. Kicking a large ball, dribbling keeping ball close and under control using either foot, later using obstacles such as skittles or bean bags.
7. Kicking against wall for speed and control.
8. Kicking for distance, chasing and controlling.
9. Hitting small ball or shuttle with stick or bat.
10. Controlling small ball with implement around obstacles and eventually partner.
11. Catching and fielding – essential practices which can be combined

with above activities especially when introducing work in pairs or groups.

12. Jumping – opportunities to practise 'how far', 'how high' with easy forms of measurement.

Section One

Practices singly: whole class activity without apparatus.

1. Free running fast, skipping on signal – run straight, short strides.
2. Running and stopping left, right, forward on signal – positive running, avoid slip step sideways.
3. Running with sudden starts and stops – include dodging.
4. Running starting slowly, work up to speed and stop fast or slow.
5. Zigzag running with quick changes of direction.
6. Short 5-to-7 stride controlled run jumping for height – essential to have reasonably short run-up – must be coached.
7. Longer run-ups jumping for distance – see surface is non-slip – coach idea of trying to jump off the same foot each time, to land on both feet.

Section Two

Practices singly with apparatus, e.g. small ball each.

1. Running and bouncing fast. Emphasize making the ball travel in all directions constantly under control.
2. Standing and running, bouncing at different heights, high and low.
3. Bouncing with right and left hand alternately on the run.
4. Race bouncing 'there' and throwing and catching back.
5. Changing freely from throwing and catching to bouncing. Beat own record in limited time.
6. Free space batting ball into air letting it rebound and hitting again. Make hand flat and get under ball. If sufficient number, use playbats at later stage.

All these practices can be repeated with *large balls*. Usually, however, it is necessary to create groups; try to keep groups to three, encouraging both skill and co-operation.

Practices singly with a ball and a bat, ball and stick – along the ground and in air.

1. Running, bouncing or dribbling.
2. Batting or hitting against a wall for speed to beat own record.

3. Batting or hitting at target on wall or at skittle placed near wall.
4. Shinty stick or hockey-stick shape, dribbling first for control at speed in any direction, later progressing to dribbling around objects.
5. Shinty stick or hockey-stick shape, driving without lifting stick higher than the shoulder, front or rear against wall, controlling rebound.

Coaching points concerning stick activities include concentration on getting hands in correct order on stick, i.e. left hand uppermost, keeping hands away from body, left elbow forward and ball in front of right foot. These are only guiding ideas. The crucial test of 'how many' is more important than 'how' particularly since encouragement and relative individual success must precede expertise.

Section Three

Practices in pairs with small ball: possible use of bats or sticks later.

1. Throwing and catching, underarm, standing, varying height, direction and speed gradually. Coach catching by wildly exaggerating reception and 'give' of the hands.
2. Roll, field, throw and catch; build up speed and direction of roll.
3. Same practices using the overarm throw – ladies may often profitably use an able boy demonstrator to show this action.
4. Same practices taken on the move and eventually at controlled speed.
5. Ball to each child: continuous simultaneous throwing and catching.
6. Running forward bouncing ball across space, later using either hands or small playbats retaining bounce but hitting back instead of catching.
7. One bouncing, turning to avoid partner intercepting. If partner intercepts he carries on bouncing.
8. Throw at wall, jump over rebound for partner to catch and immediately throw quickly changing places to continue. Count continuous successes.
9. Passing and later dribbling with either feet or stick.

Once again most of these practices are applicable to use of large ball; usually groups must be slightly larger due to lack of equipment.

Section Four

Practices with 3 or 4 and one large ball.

1. On move see how many catches can be made in given time.

2. Keeping ball up in defined area using hands, feet, head and body as situation demands.

3. Circle: throw and catch, feeding in any direction, gradually on the move.

4. Pig in the middle or 2 against 1: coach the one holding ball to stand still while throwing below head height; receiver must dodge from side to side.

5. One against 2; same coaching point. Progress to counting number of passes achieved before ball is intercepted.

6. Kicking, working to passing with control in defined area.

7. Two versus 1, or 2 versus 2 using feet and gradually allowing tackling but strictly discouraging more than two near the ball at any one moment. Possible to include objective, e.g. wall mark, skittle that either one pair attack whilst others defend, or have both pairs mutually trying to hit and defend same object.

8. Using basically same approaches, the one-handed guided netball pass, chest pass of basketball can be gradually introduced enjoyably.

Practices in threes and fours using bats, small balls, quoits.

Many practices using groups of this size can be created working from pat bouncing to keep the ball moving. Use of a rebound wall and bounces over a rope between two chairs or bench – moving very slowly towards simple competitive scoring systems.

Quoits may be used for many of the practices outlined for large ball use.

Section Five

Group practices – changing round on signal – possibly three changes per lesson.

1. Running catching large ball. Count number of catches before ball is dropped. Train everyone in group to have the ball in turn.

2. Hoop bowling, racing forward to get through, or in twos bowling to each other across space (hoop each, or in twos bowling forward changing to keep hoop moving.

3. Small ball each, throwing and catching against wall or kicking against wall or rolling ball against wall, fielding, eventually same activities in pairs.

4. Pairs – line of skittles running and bouncing and catching or throwing and catching between each gap.

5. Circle of skittles, large ball – dribbling round using inside and out-side of both feet.

6. Hockey shape, shinty stick, or long-handled bats – dribbling and driving practice towards wall mark or skittle.

7. Ropes – skipping racing style, stands and rope, jumping high prac-tice.

8. Playbats, small balls – hitting across rope or bench.

9. In threes aiming with large ball through hoop held vertically, by third child. By adding chair on which holder stands to hold hoop at arm's length horizontally, netball and basketball shooting practices can be introduced.

Section Six

'Matches' – 4 or 5 a side, using team braids to distinguish teams. Players must stay in their own area of hall or playground.

Team Passing: one large ball. Count number of consecutive catches. When the ball is dropped and picked up by the same side the score con-tinues. When the ball is picked up by the other side the score starts again. Good throwing and spacing together with emphasis on finding spaces to receive passes will be essential coaching points.

Bounce Ball: one large ball, four large hoops. Stand in twos with 'enemy' marking partner – pairs well spaced. Start with bounce between two players. Player with ball runs, bouncing ball towards a hoop to score, or if marked or touched, bounces ball to another member of his side. A team may only score once in any hoop. There is no specific direction in which to play. Clear bounce in hoop scores. Game may be started by pass – returning to centre to restart after each score with alternate sides having the centre pass-off.

Mat Ball: one large ball and small mat as goal at each end of short court. A 'catcher' stands on each mat. Remaining players stand marking in pairs freely spaced. These players run to get free and work passes towards their catcher avoiding running when they actually have the ball. En-courage short direct passing. When the ball is passed to catcher and a full catch made, the score accumulates and the game may continue by catcher throwing out or the opposing team may have pass-off from the centre. Variations of this game can easily be made by having catchers on bench so that they may more easily be seen and allowing bouncing when in possession.

Tower Ball

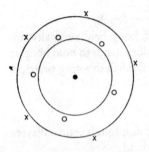

Circles marked as in diagram. Inner team defend skittle or post until it has been hit three times, teams then change places. Encourage correct throwing of large ball, and passes across or around the circle before shooting. Intercepted passes are returned to attackers.

With the same markings other useful games such as:

Wandering Ball: bean bag or small ball used, no skittle. Throwing across circle high and low. Any interception means the thrower changes place with the catcher.

Circle Dodge Football: one large ball, no skittle. Inner team must jump and dodge whilst outer team try to kick the ball to hit them below waist.

Small-Side Games Using Rounders Type Pitch

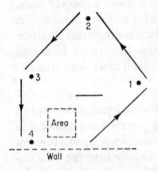

Beat the Ball: large playbat, playball. Batsman strikes ball and then attempts to complete circuit before ball is fielded and passed to each post in turn.

Tunnel Ball Rounders: same equipment, but at each strike the fielders line up behind team leader or bowler if preferred and the ball is passed through the tunnel formed by their legs before the runner reaches home.

Football Rounders: ball is rolled by hand after which it is always propelled by foot. The 'batsman' attempts to run round the bases before the ball is returned to a marked area.

Small-Side Games Using Long Narrow Pitches

Scoring wicket

Batsman

Bowler

or

Bowler

Non-stop Cricket: bat shape, tennis ball, wickets or wall. Striker runs round post or touches mark 10 yds to left of wicket. Ball returned and bowled even if he or she is absent. Striker must run when he hits ball.

Non-stop Stoolball: same game using large playbat and either tennis ball or playball and some form of stoolball wicket at suitable height for players.

Longball: rectangular pitch marked by wickets or posts. Ball is struck by playbat or hand into area bounded by posts. To score, whole team run from striking end to beyond line of far wickets and back without being hit with the ball. Fielders are not allowed to run with the ball but are allowed to throw it to team-mate more favourably placed.

Small-Side Team Games Using Small Rectangular Areas

Since these activities are most active and enjoyable played in pairs, two adjoining areas of approximately the same size will be needed to accommodate 6 or 8 players. Exact court sizes are unnecessary at this stage, and benches or rope may be used to indicate position and height of net. If multi-purpose posts are available, narrow nets are inexpensive and can be erected by the children.

1. Tenniquoits: rubber or rope quoit, net at approximately 4 ft 6 in. Serve diagonally, return quoit without excessive foot movement. Score: twelve to fifteen points a game, using either tennis system, table tennis system or any local system which the children can easily understand.

2. Padder Tennis: playbats, tennis or gamester ball, bench or if available net at approximate height of 2 ft to 2 ft 3 in. As before choose most easily

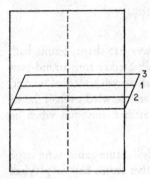

understood system of scoring available – or if possible dispense with scoring altogether and play for fun.

3. *Batinton:* playbats, shuttle, net at approximately 5 ft; needs much practice before scoring is introduced.

Small-Side Team Games Using Larger Rectangular Areas

The early stages of the major games in some ways present considerable difficulties for future improvement due to the fact that if left free to individual experiment children may acquire 'habits of skill' which will interfere with later progress. In each case, therefore, the teacher should insist on certain essential features known to be required later to be present from the beginning. Examples of such skills are the avoidance of 'sticks' and turning in both shinty and hockey – both practices which if perfected will later have to be eradicated. The really essential features of any major game, plus the inculcation of good manners, i.e. avoidance of noise and argument, gestures of over-exultation and particularly selfish play really need be the only guide lines. Selfish players are often very keen and may well be cured by the creation of a 'two-minute sin bin' system – arbitrarily but fairly operated.

Shinty: shinty sticks, 4-in. or 7-in. playball, developing gradually to soft-cored pudding-type ball and eventually to tennis ball especially on hard surface areas. On grass areas the wooden shinty ball may prove more satisfactory.

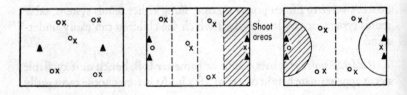

Earliest stages: skittles for goals, start with centre pass, must be near skittle to shoot, push strokes only – avoid raising stick more than waist high – roll in from side and ends.

Later (as soon as possible): introduce centre bully and defined shooting areas, allowing the newly introduced goalkeeper to prevent scoring with stick, hand or foot.

Constant insistence on passing and team play in the early stages will prove very beneficial to both progress and nerves as time goes by.

Hockey: hockey-stick shapes, same ball progression as shinty. Striking with one side of the stick only must be enforced, if necessary painting the hitting side of the shape (allowing for the left-handed children). Sticks and turning must also be avoided, and features such as simple centre bully, roll in, defined shooting areas and goalkeeper introduced as soon as possible. Simple corners and roll-in lines may also be incorporated at the very latest stages with particularly able classes.

To achieve any success at either shinty or hockey they must be played on fairly true surfaces, i.e. in most Primary schools hard areas such as playgrounds. Where suitable grass areas are available the following pitch marking could serve as a guide to be altered to suit local conditions or individual experience.

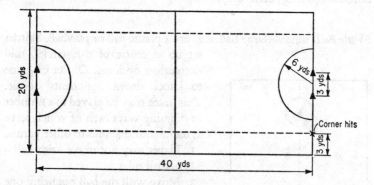

Doddery Rugby: size 3 or 4 plastic rugby ball, preferably played on grass or in mid playground away from walls. Stands either multi-purpose, high jump or home-made and two hoops.

Running in any direction preferably towards opponents' line, pass in any direction when touched. Stop, look around and pass below head

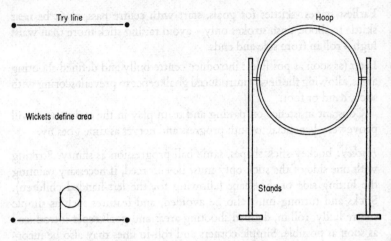

height to a team-mate. Score by grounding ball beyond opponents' end line without having first been touched – 2 points. From previously determined point in front of hoop throw for goal. If successful add further point.

Game started by pass from centre, no kicking. As soon as possible introduce passing 'back' only.

Skittle Ball: suitable large ball, e.g. size 4 plastic ball or playball. Skittles set up at centre of 6-ft circles, mid dotted line optional. Object of game to knock down opponents' skittle. This game may be played in a number of differing ways each of which serve as useful introductions to other games.

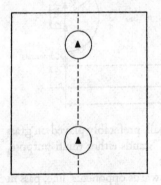

1. Player may not move with ball – netball rules.

2. Move with the ball bouncing one hand– basketball rules.

3. Run until touched – doddery rugby.

Whichever way it is played it is capable of producing great enjoyment provided a recognized system is constantly used. When played outdoors it is often wise to have each team change the goalkeeper from time to time.

Netball: size 4 plastic ball, netball stands either portable, bracketed from wall or home-made with ring fixed at approximately 6 ft to 7 ft so that many goals can be scored.

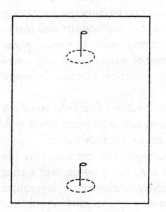

Start with pass from centre and from the beginning encourage minimum travelling when in possession, and short, low, well directed passes to team-mates who are constantly on the move. Discourage rough play particularly robbing the ball and allow any player who is in possession of the ball near the post to shoot for goal without interruption from opposition. Play all round post and if possible create shooting circle to define shooting area.

Unless short, low, correct passes are vigorously enforced the game will develop poorly due to the understandable desire of small children to pass through the stratosphere.

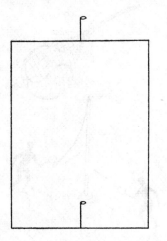

Basketball: size 4 plastic ball or large playball. Goals for this game at this stage can be created as originally by suspending baskets at 6 ft to 7 ft from posts or better still use netball fittings ignoring the backboard.

Start the game with centre pass after which any player may pass or dribble the ball with one hand in any direction. From the beginning it must be understood that after a dribble ends i.e. the ball is held in both hands it must be passed or a shot at goal taken. Opponents may try to intercept passes or shots but may not attempt to take the ball away from the child in possession. Avoid personal contact at all times, and encourage passing and shooting. Restart game after score by pass from end line by defenders. Score 2 points for each successful shot.

Soccer: size 4 plastic ball or if preferred and available size 3 or 4 football. Posts for grass areas preferably portable either on base or capable of being pushed into the ground; for hard areas use standing posts or wall markings. Great emphasis on passing, running into spaces to receive passes and shooting with positive discouragement of shouting, arguing, over-enthusiastic physical violence and any tendency towards excessive emotion after scoring.

Many rules such as off-side, direct and indirect free kicks and even penalties can be ignored, being resorted to and introduced when such heinous crimes as 'forgetful handling in the goalmouth' occur.

Correct throwing in from touch, kick-offs and corners, plus the occasional exhortations to pass, spread out, and play-on will suffice almost *ad infinitum.* Due to intensive parental encouragement, playground and free-time practice, the juvenile expert may at times prove a problem. Possible solutions include a heart to heart talk, the two-minute sin bin, and if fortunate enough to have 8 or 10 such experts, group them together leaving true ability to bloom whilst merely controlling the noise and behaviour level.

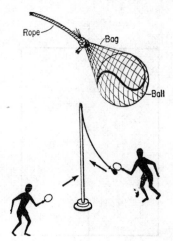

Bumble-puppy: previously well known in some areas of the country, this very useful and interesting game is now more available due to the availability of specially made equipment. In the games sense it has the marked advantage that the area required is both small and exact. It can therefore be used to fill up those 'odd' areas of playground which are too small for other 'miniature games'.

Bumble-puppy stand consists of post 6 ft to 7 ft long, to the top of which a length of light rope is fixed. At the free end of the rope a tennis ball contained in small open string bag is fastened.

The object of the game which may be played as singles or doubles is to hit the tennis ball until the rope is completely wrapped round the post in your hitting direction.

The equipment is quite easy to produce locally, using a post in the ground or on a stand, and getting a parent to tat or crochet a bumble-puppy bag to hold the tennis ball.

For safety's sake it is usual to play using playbats but small string rackets can be used especially for singles.

Relays

Whole class 4 or 5 a side 'matches' under controlled conditions suitable both for indoor and outdoor use can be interpreted as relays which are particularly suited to children of this age. Much enjoyment, friendly competition and useful skill practice can be taught in this fashion provided the relays chosen keep inactivity to a minimum.

To make relays worth while the following points must be observed:

(a) Teams must be even in number (make odd ones judges; if three join in yourself).

(b) Front and back lines must be drawn.

(c) Instructions must be clear. If necessary walk the whole class through the relay to be performed.

(d) Even out the ability between teams if constant winners occur.

(e) Keep teams small and use scoring system to help competition.

(f) Avoid relays in which only one member of the team is active at a time.

(g) Only use relays when the standard of skill required for the relay chosen has reached a level at which its performance at speed by the majority is obviously possible. Early relays will mainly be concerned with the whole body skills of running, hopping, skipping and dodging.

(h) Teach fast start, readiness to go, exercise of control at turning points to avoid over running, waste of time and derision and despairing cries of team.

Resourceful teachers can adapt relays to stimulate practice in any particular direction that requires attention. Usually the simpler the form the greater the actual physical activity, but as the children become more able to manipulate games equipment the relays can be made more complicated by adding all types of apparatus and obstacles.

Examples of Possible Relays and Formations (based on 4 children per team)
  Note: the same space is required for 9 teams of 4 as for 4 teams of 9, but the practice and activity achieved by turning the teams sideways is infinitely greater.

A. Short File formation   ●   ●   ●   ●

Single action – all involved relays using large ball

Tunnel Ball: all feet astride, ball rolled through tunnel guided or assisted by team members. Last member of team picks up ball races to front, team move back one place – repeat.

Over the Head: ball is passed back over the head, each member of the team must catch and pass, brought to front and repeated as in tunnel ball.

Over and Under: leader always passes ball through legs, next child over the head and then alternately, last child bringing ball to front and passing ball under legs having reached front line.

These three simple relays can be invigorated by adding 'straddling', i.e. last player bringing ball to front by straddling over backs of team who have crouched down immediately they have sent the ball on its way to the rear in the appropriate fashion. Other additions such as tunnel ball 'five' times through, and eventually when the relays are very well known a combination of all three, i.e. tunnel ball twice, over the head twice and over and under twice could be used.

All Action – all involved relays using this formation – no apparatus.

First of all, these relays will have to be walked through several times so that their unusual pattern may be learned. Once this pattern is acquired it can be used for a variety of differing activities used singly, in pairs or in combinations.

Method: e.g. In and Out Relay, team of 4.

On 'Go', back team member starts going in and out those in front, as he passes number 3 he immediately follows, as 4 and then 3 pass 2 he joins in, when number 4 passes team leader he turns right and runs straight back to his place closely followed by 3, 2 and 1 who has started when passed by 2. Numbers 3, 2 and 1 go round the back man and going in and out stop when they return to their original position.

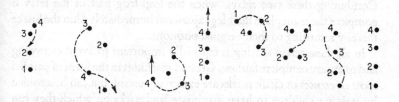

Other relays which may be used with the 'all-in' type of formation are:

Leap Frog Relay: avoid backs being too low since 'unfair' practice will soon be noted and vociferously commented upon by other teams.

Straddle Relay: this time team get low so that team-mates can straddle over without jumping. Teach tight crouch avoiding elbows protruding and wide fast straddling.

Under the Legs: feet wide apart – crawl or slide under on all fours between.

Over the Legs: start sitting legs stretched out straight, go over team-mates' legs. Teach fast sit down with straight legs to avoid oncoming runners catching toes under bent knees.

Same formation – other ideas
Continuous Leap Frog: the last player leap frogs over the rest, the others following as passed. The file progresses in a straight line over a given space.

Skin the Snake: file stands with legs apart. On the signal the leader turns and goes through the legs of the second person who is then free to follow the leader and so on.

Continuous Leap Frog and Skin the Snake

Combining these two relays, when the leap frog part of the relay is complete the team place their legs apart and immediately Skin the Snake thereby returning to their original positions.

In all these relays spacing is especially important to avoid crowding and to ensure complete fairness. Ground markings in the form of painted spots or crosses or chalk marks are extremely useful, but can be avoided by training children to have inanimate landmarks on which they can quickly check their position.

A. Short File formation (leader facing group)

$$ \underset{1}{\bullet} \dashleftarrow \dashrightarrow \underset{2}{\bullet} \qquad \underset{3}{\bullet} \qquad \underset{4}{\bullet} $$

A useful formation for a number of throwing and catching skills with small balls, large balls bean bags and quoits, since it obliges the children to throw and catch accurately over varying distances constantly.

Basically the leader faces the team and throws in any designated way, e.g. chest pass with large ball, or shoulder pass or soccer throw-in to first player who returns ball in same manner and then crouches down. The same procedure is followed to number 2, but when number 3 receives the ball it is brought to the front, while the team jump up moving back one place to allow previous thrower to take his place at front.

Many additions are possible such as whole team run to touch designated point when the last player receives the ball each time, returning to start next cycle.

B. Corner Spry Formation

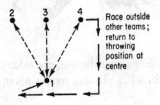

Race outside other teams; return to throwing position at centre

In this formation hitting and kicking activities can be added to throwing, and additional running may be incorporated which often adds interest.

Example: leader with large ball stands facing team ready to do bounce pass relay passes to 2 and 3 who bounce pass back – then to 4 who receiving the ball races round rear of other teams or to designated spot bouncing or carrying the ball and returns to centre to repeat process. During his absence number 1 takes number 2's place and remaining players move one place to left so that for the next repeat number 3 is at running position.

This type of formation can be varied in arrangement, throwing, hitting or kicking distance according to necessity.

C. Shuttle or Exchange Formation

All types of activities can be incorporated with ease into this formation, the greatest problem may well be counting how many times the team has repeated an activity rather than any organizational or manipulative difficulty.

In the early stages many teachers may prefer to have their running, hopping, dodging, bouncing with hand or bat, hoop rolling, dribbling with hand, foot, stick or bat from the short file formation. As skill increases these activities can be speeded up and made more challenging by adopting this shuttle or exchange formation.

Teams are halved in number and placed so that the halves face each other across a defined and preferably marked space. Simple relays such as running, hopping, skipping will establish in the children's minds the fact that they have completed one complete cycle when they are all back to their starting position.

Possibilities for relays using shuttle formation.

1. Running.
2. Hopping.
3. Jumping with both feet.
4. Rabbit jumping.
5. Skipping.
6. Hoop bowling.

7. Bouncing large ball, small ball using one hand.
8. Bouncing using bats and small balls.
9. Dribbling using inside of feet – ball kept close.
10. Dribbling using shinty stick.
11. Dribbling using hands and large ball.
12. Run and pass – rugby ball, soccer ball.

In almost every case one can add obstacles such as skittles, bean bags, ropes, supported canes or hoops as required to emphasize some other feature which you wish either to introduce or which happens to be a noted weakness of the group.

By selection from the activities suggested in each of the foregoing sections lessons can be planned to suit this age-range taking into account facilities, equipment, time and the previous experience of the children on the lines of Form A previously outlined.

Form B – Alternative Lesson Plan

Individual differences and preferences occur just as much in teachers as in children although they tend to receive far less publicity. The same activities will obviously be involved to a great extent as previously outlined, but the slightly simpler framework in which they are presented may help some teachers, especially during those terrible moments which most teachers experience at least once when the mind goes blank and one wonders 'what on earth comes next'.

Lesson Form B

| Introductory |
| Running and Chasing games |
| Partner activities |
| Group activities |
| Relays or Team games |

Introductory: decide what apparatus is to be available and whether free choice is to operate. Practices can be individual or paired, covering ball, rope, bat and ball, shinty stick and ball, hockey shape and ball, cricket bat shape and ball, and hoop activities and including work without apparatus.

Running: activities as in Section 1, Form A, p. 22.

Chasing Games: all forms of 'Tag', and other games such as Dodge and Mark and Free and Caught.

Partner Activities: painted lines are useful – 60 ft for throwing, 30 ft for bouncing and hitting.

1. Throwing and catching.
2. Bounce and catch.
3. Bowling to pitch to catcher.
4. Dribbling around partner.
5. Dribbling using sticks – shinty or hockey.
6. Returning bounced ball with playbat.
7. Heading – light ball.
8. Passing by hand on the move – feet, hands, sticks.

Paired shuttle relays can often be used to stimulate greater speed in this phase.

Timing can be adapted to time available and emphasis preferred.

Group Activities: activities as in Section 3, Form A, p. 23, can be used for this section, or choice of eight from the following suggestions, using challenges:

Apparatus	*Challenge*
1. Skittles, 2½-in. balls or playballs	'Use your feet'
2. Wall marks, 2½-in. sorbo balls	Aiming and catching practice
3. Skittles, and cane, ash stave with rubber foot	'Pole yourself over'
4. Size 4 light plastic balls	Heading practice
5. Tennis, gamester or sorbo 2½-in. balls and playbats	'Keep it up' – standing and moving
6. Variety of 2½-in. balls	'Ways of throwing and catching'
7. Playground wickets or wall mark	Aiming and bowling
8. Shinty sticks, balls, skittles	Free practice – dribbling, hitting
9. Bats, balls, rope, skittles	'Make up a game'
10. Jumping stands, size 4 plastic ball	'Make up a hand or heading game'
11. Jumping stands, bats, shuttle	'Make up a hitting game'
12. Jumping stands, quoit, hoop, rope	'Make up a game'
13. Netball post, size 4 plastic ball	2 v. 2 – one way goal
14. Skittle in 6-ft circle	4 v. 1 – 'Defend the tower'
15. Circle, playball	Circle dodge ball 3 v. 1 kicking
16. Graded chalk lines	'How far can you broad jump?'
17. Jumping stands, mats, rope	'How high can you jump?'

18. 2 v. 2: retaining possession of ball whether dribbling, hand passing,

heading, shinty or hockey dribbling. Coach that one not in possession moves into space.

19. 2 *v*. 1: 'Pig in the Middle' – training for most games. Shows that two should outwit one. The pig tries to intercept.

20. 3 *v*. 2: Coach moving into space to receive and keen interception. The three should in theory beat the two.

Relays or Miniature Games: refer to previous sections for choice of activities.

Chapter 4: Background Information

Facilities and Time Allocation

These two factors are so often closely linked that it would appear sensible to consider them at the same time.

Indoor facilities vary greatly from school to school, and many are far from ideal for games purposes. The ideal would be a school hall of adequate size uncluttered by stages, platforms, chairs, bookcases, dinner-tables, television sets and school trophies to be available for every P.E. period shown on the timetable. The minimum requirement is its availability for one period per week for each class, increasing this allocation wherever possible especially for the younger children.

Even the minimum requirement cannot be achieved in many cases and one must therefore face the fact that most of these lessons will be taken out of doors. This may be a blessing in disguise since in the majority of cases they are outdoor activities in their full form.

Since other physical aspects appear on the timetable it is suggested that most of the games training as outlined will take place outdoors in two major 'blocks' namely September, October and November and in the late Spring Term and the Summer Term. This may not be ideal but it is practical, since little learning is achieved outdoors during rain, fog and other types of miserable weather. During this period indoor spaces could well block gymnastics, music and movement and dance which would in their turn taper off when better weather occurs

If each child of this age receives a period of physical activity of some kind daily throughout the school year, with our present facilities one can ask no more.

Changing

Children can work effectively and safely only if suitably clothed and shod. They should be trained from earliest days to remove the maximum amount of clothing consistent with the weather and floor surface conditions. Indoors the temptation to perform in socks, or tights must be stifled at birth since accidents can arise especially during quick movements. Gym shoes or bare feet should be the rule indoors, and gym shoes out of doors.

Teachers should set the class a standard in this respect by always changing into gym shoes before taking a games lesson. It is surprising how looking the part often helps over a period of time to affect class changing and some teachers' confidence to take such lessons.

Hygiene

Realizing that changing time at each end of games lessons can reduce teaching time by at least eight minutes even in well organized classes, and realizing the lack of washing facilities, for large numbers simultaneously in many schools it is little wonder that hygiene is neglected after games lessons in many schools.

Difficult though it may be to arrange and supervise, any teacher who takes a little more off the teaching time to inculcate the habit of washing the hands and face and giving the perspiring body a thorough rub down with a personal towel will render the individual and the community a great and necessary service.

Safety Factors

1. Plan (especially indoors) to avoid obstructions, running towards walls or confined spaces.
2. Outdoors, have very strict rules about procedure when missiles find their way off the school premises especially where roads, the school roof and private property are concerned.
3. Quickly check that all children are correctly shod every lesson. Do not allow participation in socks indoors or ordinary shoes outdoors.
4. Use equipment which is of correct size and weight for age group. Beware use of heavy skittles as goal posts.
5. ALWAYS BE PRESENT.
6. Know the L.E.A. accident procedure, including site of telephone, number required – stop the remainder of the class, attend to injured child, keeping warm and reassured until professional assistance is available.

Games Apparatus

There should be sufficient apparatus to equip all classes which may be at work at the same time. Items such as small balls, skipping ropes, bean bags, quoits, etc., should be stored in equal quantities in team boxes or light wire mesh baskets. Keeping coloured equipment in the same coloured box or cage greatly assists return and checking of equipment. Schools which have more than one class working at a time may have to duplicate certain items. Co-operation between the teachers concerned can avoid the necessity of doubling quantities and can achieve best and fullest use of all apparatus.

Priorities

Suggested order of priority where finance is limited would be:
(i) Small balls. (ii) Skipping ropes. (iii) Large plastic or rubber balls. (iv) Playbats and gamester balls. (v) Skittles and canes. (vi) Hoops, quoits, shuttles. (vii) Shinty sticks, hockey and cricket shapes. (viii) Ash staves. (ix) Pudding balls.

Many authorities have funds with which they are able to assist schools purchase items such as playground wickets, jumping stands, netball posts, basketball stands and multi-purpose apparatus. For such items it is well to approach the local authority to inquire whether any such assistance is possible before launching out on any great expenditure.

A guide to purchase with very approximate costs would be as follows:

Item	Size	Cost	Comments
1. *Small Balls*			
Solid Sorbo	2½″	16s doz.	Invaluable for catching, throwing and bouncing. Beware picking – need at least one each – probably 4 dozen.
Hollow rubber	2½″	10s doz.	Useful for bat activities – could be alternative to Sorbo, otherwise 2 dozen.
Tennis ball	2½″	30s doz.	Best all-purpose ball still – acquire locally from devious sources. Available uncovered – cheap and useful.
Plastic perforated gamester	2½″	13s doz.	Particularly suitable for indoor use since avoids breakage of windows. Useful to have 2 dozen 2½-inch.
	3½″	22s doz.	
	5¼″	43s doz.	
Storage net	—	5s	Best stored dispersed in team baskets or free carrot sack.

Item	Size	Cost	Comments
2. *Skipping Ropes*			
Infants: Jute	7–8'	14s doz.	Having chosen size and mater-
Cotton	7–8'	19s doz.	ial will need one per child plus
Juniors: Jute	8–9'	16s doz.	spares, i.e. 4 dozen, with two
Cotton	8–9'	22s doz.	long ropes for use as nets in
Long Ropes	15–21'	45s each	many situations. Insist on correct storage.
3. *Large Plastic Balls*			
Frido vinyl	8½" 8½ oz	5s to 6s	Good for throwing, heading – 1 dozen.
Frido-master	8½" 16 oz	8s to 9s	Kicking, throwing – 1 dozen.
Moulded rubber football/netball	3	40s	Sizes 3 and 4 suitable – expen-
	4	42s	sive but durable – except for
	5	44s	matches or rallies. Possibly 2 of each size.
4. *Playbats (built-up handles)*			
Table tennis shape		2s each	Used for many activities.
Round face	6–7" faces		Assorted stock of 4 dozen
Butter pat shape		1s 6d each	– 10 each basket, 8 spares in stock.
5. *Skittles*			
Variety of shapes, grooved tops	12"×3"×3"	4s 6d each	Used for goals, hurdling, jump- ing – 24 would cover most requirements.
Canes	6–7'	9s doz.	Two dozen – 18 available – 6 stored.
New Skittle Activity skittle		17s 3d each	Plastic covered – light – easy to store – capable of holding canes at various heights and support- ing hoops firmly in vertical and horizontal positions. Re- commended purchase when re-stocking.
6. *Hoops*			
Plastic coloured	18"	65s doz.	One per child of varying sizes
	24"	79s doz.	used as designed, skipping, hula
	30"	95s doz.	goals – 4 dozen.
	36"	110s doz.	
Storage stand	100 hoops	60s	Well worth acquiring.
Quoits			
Sorbo rubber		35s doz.	One dozen.

Item	Size	Cost	Comments
Shuttles			
Plastic preferred	—	—	Few purchased or better still acquired locally will suffice.
7. *Shinty Sticks*	—	5s each	Two dozen.
Balls	2½–3⅛″	3s each	Use tennis or pudding ball on hard areas.
Hockey shapes	—	14s each	One dozen.
Cricket bat shapes	3	8s each	Building up to 3 of each size to accommodate all shapes and sizes and to have a spare available.
	4	8s 6d each	
	5	9s each	
	6	9s 3d each	
Pudding balls	4¾ oz	10s each	Suitable for shinty, hockey, cricket – 6.
8. *Ash Staves*			
Rubber foot	5′ × 1¾″	9s each	3 or 4.
	6′ × 1½″	16s each	If purchased – 3 or 4 would suffice.
Other Items			
(*a*) Rugby balls	4	7s 3d each	Useful to have 3 or 4.
(*b*) Bean bags	6″ × 4″	35s doz.	One dozen usually sufficient at this stage.
(*c*) Stilts	5′ steel	42s pair	Available in wood – 2 or 3 pairs.
(*d*) Team braid	1″ wide	5s 4d doz yds	Often essential – personal choice of material.
	1½″ wide	9s doz yds	
	Plastic	8s doz.	
(*e*) Storage baskets	24″ × 14″ × 12″	45s each	4 essential – 6 often useful.
(*f*) Storage trolley	—	—	Including 4 baskets, hoop stand, cane stand – £18.
(*g*) Playground wickets	Junior	19s 6d	Very useful – 2 pairs.

Larger Apparatus

Most Junior schools very logically use apparatus such as netball posts for all the age-ranges from 7 to 11. In recent years however to accommodate the wider scope of games now covered in Junior schools 'multi-purpose' apparatus has been put on market which is particularly appropriate to many of the activities outlined for this age group. It has the marked advantages of being of a more suitable height, much more portable and far safer to move about especially for younger children. To headteachers it has the marked advantage that it is far easier to store and covers a variety of activities by one purchase. Since it is obviously more expensive than the small equipment previously listed inquiries through the local organizer should preceed fund raising or even home-made equipment on these lines.

The following diagrams give some idea of the equipment and its uses:

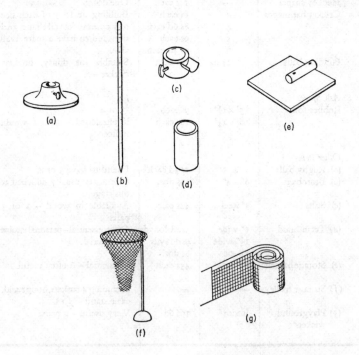

(a) Metal bases, grooved to take post with locking nut – approximately 35s each.

(b) Metal posts marked for height measurement with spiked ends for use on grass without bases. Usually 4 ft to 4 ft 6 in. long – approximately 35s each.

(c) Jumping slides for use with posts – hold cane or rope – approximately 20s a pair.

(*d*) Wooden post extension enabling nets to be fixed at heights up to 5 ft – useful for battinton, volleyball – approximately 20s each,

(*e*) Regulation adjustable stoolball wickets, any height – approximately 25s each.

(*f*) Netball ring and extension to fit on top of post – 6 ft – approximately 58s a pair. Extremely useful for introducing adapted netball and basketball.

(*g*) Ten-foot net easily attached to posts at any height suitable – approximately 16s 6d each for introducing padder, batinton, tennis, quoits, etc.

A wide selection of activities can be catered for by purchasing four bases, posts, stoolball wickets and jumping slides: and two jumping ropes, games nets and two pairs of netball rings at a total approximate cost of £30.

Class Organization

Having acquired all the equipment, planned the lesson, taken all safety factors into consideration, and become acquainted with accident procedure the teacher can lighten his load by involving the children in the organization in the following ways:

1. Equipment Monitors: responsible for taking out equipment and placing it ready for use. Check lists enable children to report any deficiencies. Change per half term – spread feeling of importance.

2. Rotation Monitors: full rotation of all groups is usually impossible – children note where groups should start next time after home app. is out.

Finally a practice which prevents much explanation out of doors, when the children are eager to be busy; spend a few moments before leaving the classroom telling the class what they will be doing in the forthcoming lesson.

Stubborn insistence on changing and other important organizational factors in the early weeks will pay handsome dividends during the year. Decide on the procedures and the rules and within the bounds of reason and human understanding enforce them unless a better arrangement grows upon you through experience.

Chapter 5: Upper Juniors

Due to early maturation and obvious natural games ability, a great deal of overlap often occurs between the Lower and Upper Junior stages. As a general rule it is in the Upper Junior stage when more orthodox games lessons should appear. Class and group practices will now be directly geared to a particular game suitably adapted where necessary to suit the games 'feeling' of children of this age.

A simple method of planning such lessons in outline is shown by the following diagram which seeks to balance skills teaching and actual play

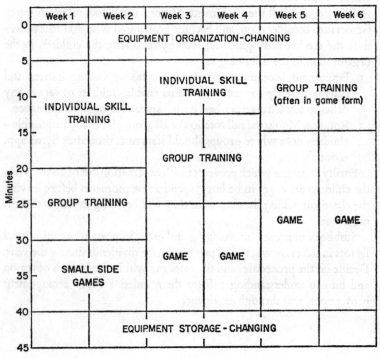

	Week 1	Week 2	Week 3	Week 4	Week 5	Week 6
0	EQUIPMENT ORGANIZATION – CHANGING					
5	INDIVIDUAL SKILL TRAINING		INDIVIDUAL SKILL TRAINING		GROUP TRAINING (often in game form)	
10						
15			GROUP TRAINING			
20	GROUP TRAINING					
25					GAME	GAME
30			GAME	GAME		
35	SMALL SIDE GAMES					
40						
45	EQUIPMENT STORAGE – CHANGING					

in a 6-week (i.e. half term) block. Although many may prefer to work on the simple and effective scheme of one-third skills, two-thirds play, the type of progression and planning suggested here has much to recommend it and would be well worth trying by many teachers.

All the games which follow can easily be fitted into a scheme of work based on this form of outline plan.

Junior schools have the great advantage that games seasons need not be a very limiting factor in their planning. If they wish they can play and teach a variety of games throughout the year, or adapt their programme to the vagaries of the weather, e.g. hockey in the summer, net games in early autumn. Quite rightly they are the sole arbiters of what they choose to attempt. Two great factors must be borne in mind, however, when viewing the results of the pattern used, namely: were the majority of the children TAUGHT as distinct from being allowed to play, and have they been presented with opportunities of trying a sufficient variety of games to enable them to approach future skill learning with increase d confidence.

Interschool competitions are often well established and organized in many areas, which give great meaning to skill learning of certain games, and as on the whole they are wisely run, they have beneficial effects. They should not, however, be allowed to be the sole determinant of the games programme planning, since the 'many' may be sacrificed for the good of the few.

Soccer

Many areas are encouraging the coaching and playing of soccer in Junior schools in units of six, both within the school and in the form of rallies at which every school plays every other school competing. Many schools, previously unable to raise teams, have been able to join in these rallies where the main emphasis has very rightly been on activity and enjoyment.

This game has become such a dominating feature of our national life that in places where six-a-side has been taken up, the enthusiasm of the children has prompted many female teachers to inquire whether they are capable of producing a team since they are without male assistance. Results have shown that with a framework of information thorough preparation and the use of wall charts (where necessary), very successful teams and highly enjoyable lessons in this essentially male preserve can be produced by the ladies without necessarily either demonstrating or being acquainted with any of the latest formation fads.

This modified form of the major game provides a genuine play feature, its main element being end-to-end attacking play, the child's version of what football should really be like. They are satisfied with a small space, a few players, simple rules and a relatively short but highly vigorous duration of play. The game caters for their enthusiastic endeavours, immature skill and overwhelming desire to kick the ball as hard and as often as possible. From the teacher's point of view incidental coaching of positional play and discouragement of the 'herd' instinct round the ball becomes a great deal easier.

In areas which have Junior leagues strongly established, and representative teams, the keenest teachers are already often over-committed and it would be unrealistic to ask them to suddenly completely change to six-a-side, or to add an extra burden and imposition on their free time. There would, however, appear to be little difficulty in changing the form of the games lesson in school time towards skill training followed by small side games rather than one or one and a half large games. Knowing how strong some teachers' feelings are on this particular matter and respecting their convictions and endeavours it is still axiomatic that *all children have an equal right to an adequate share of play, practice and coaching, and any system which does not cater for every boy is without sound educational base.*

Section I
Apparatus recommended
Footballs

    (a) 16-oz. Frido – sizes 3 and 4.

    (b) Gamesmaster – sizes 3 and 4.

    (c) Leather – size 3.

    (d) Light Frido or playball – introduction to heading.

Aim to have at least one ball to three boys, and if possible one between two. The lighter plastic ball is unsatisfactory since it is too easily diverted by the wind but it is very suitable for netball and some basketball practices and for introducing heading in a pain-free way.

Posts

    (a) Primary soccer posts, i.e. 2 ft × 6 ft uprights and an 18-ft crossbar are often best made locally.

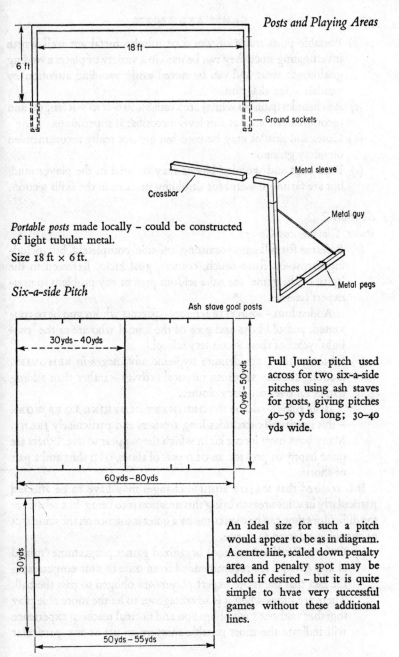

18 ft

6 ft

Ground sockets

Metal sleeve

Crossbar

Metal guy

Portable posts made locally – could be constructed of light tubular metal.

Size 18 ft × 6 ft.

Metal pegs

Six-a-side Pitch

Ash stave goal posts

30 yds – 40 yds

50 yds – 50 yds

40 yds – 50 yds

Full Junior pitch used across for two six-a-side pitches using ash staves for posts, giving pitches 40–50 yds long; 30–40 yds wide.

60 yds – 80 yds

30 yds

An ideal size for such a pitch would appear to be as in diagram. A centre line, scaled down penalty area and penalty spot may be added if desired – but it is quite simple to hvae very successful games without these additional lines.

50 yds – 55 yds

(b) Portable posts made of wood or tubular metal are well worth investigating since they can be used in a variety of places avoiding goalmouth wear and can be stored easily avoiding attention by vandals – see diagram.

(c) Ash handles (painted white) are available in 6-ft to 7-ft lengths and recommended since at this level a crossbar is superfluous.

(d) Canes and skittles may be used but are not really recommended on safety grounds.

(e) Bean bags and wooden blocks may be used in the playground, but are far more useful for dribbling practice in the skills section.

Section 2
Rules, Clothing and Groups

(a) *Rules:* as for full game omitting 'off-side' completely, but including throw-ins from touch, corners, goal kicks. Refereed in the 'spirit of the game' the rules seldom present any problem to non-expert referees.

Addendum – sources of referees – parents whom you have converted, and old boys and girls of the school who are in the 'twilight' years of their Secondary school.

(b) *Clothing:* there are definite hygienic advantages in REMOVING clothing for any vigorous physical activity – rather than adding games kit over ordinary clothes.

Basic rule should be NO ORDINARY CLOTHING TO BE WORN – this specifically excludes long trousers and particularly JEANS. Many boys have soccer kit in which they appear to live, others are quite happy to provide an OLD pair of shoes, OLD shirt and a pair of shorts.

It is realized that MAJOR attitude changes may have to be affected particularly in some areas to bring this situation into being, but whatever the difficulties they can be overcome by a quiet insistence on the standards of changing referred to above.

(c) *Groups:* Within the school organized games programme 'mixed ability groups' are recommended from time to time emphasizing the fact that the more expert players are obliged to pass the ball. There are times when it is advantageous to let the more able play together without such obligation and normal teaching experience will indicate the most suitable mixture to use at any particular time There are advantages to be gained from mixed ability groups: particularly when over-individualism is controlled and the right balance is struck between competition and co-operation in the variety of abilities involved.

Section 3
Practices
Working rules:
1. NO HANDS.
2. BALL ALWAYS KEPT ON OR NEAR THE GROUND.

A. Kicking (in pairs or threes)
At first without instruction; confining each group to an area of the field, or if in playground section of wall for rebound kicking. Gradually indicating better methods; more control and direction.

B. Stopping (in pairs or threes)
Controlling the ball before returning it – this is the basis of trapping the ball. Variety can be introduced by using either foot, shins, and even body. Later for deliberate trapping practice a partner may feed the ball by foot or hand.

C. Passing (in pairs or threes)
Originally standing facing; trying to pass at controlled speed. Gradually passing on the move – emphasizing the necessity of the ball arriving at a reasonable speed just in front of the partner.

Activities Covering Kicking, Stopping, Passing
(a) Kicking stationary ball.
(b) Kicking stationary ball increasing distance.
(c) Kicking moving ball.
(d) Kicking with non-dominant foot.
(e) Kicking at target, e.g. ash stave or chair in twos or threes.
(f) Kicking, stopping, etc., in pairs – counting hits on ash stave from 5 yds – 8 yds in 1, 2, 3, 4 minutes introducing mild inter-group competition.
(g) Using kicking board, or wall below 2 ft from ground – number of kicks achieved from 3 yds to 10 yds in stated number of minutes. Competition in that each boy competes against his own previous best score.

(h) Passing – two against one; encourage boy without ball to run into open space, boy with ball to hold, look and then pass deliberately – as skill increases the number of completed passes can be counted.

(i) Passing to beat opponent – deliberate practice of two players approaching and beating defender.

(j) Three against 3 passing within the penalty area – emphasizing moving into the empty space.

(k) Attack v. Defence – four attackers against three defenders and a goalkeeper; changing over from time to time.

(l) KICKING CRICKET – full details of this game and its related Heading Cricket both suitable for either field or playground will be found on a separate page.

D. Dribbling

After class instruction on individual lines emphasizing control, use of inside and outside of foot; walking building up to running. This essential skill can often best be practised as a group activity whilst other groups practise other skills.

Activities Emphasizing Dribbling

(a) Dribbling round object(s), e.g. bean bag(s), etc., outside foot.

(b) Dribbling round object(s), e.g. bean bag(s), etc., inside foot.

(c) Dribbling round object(s), e.g. bean bag(s), etc., either foot.

(d) Dribbling round circle of canes.

(e) Relay games – (i) straight distance dribble, (ii) shuttle relay dribbling, (iii) dribble, stop, push pass – shuttle, (iv) corner spry dribbling.

E. Shooting

Using established goals, staves or even canes, in groups of three or four this practice gives great satisfaction since cause and success are so closely linked.

The essential point of aiming to AVOID the goalkeeper has often to be stressed. In the early stages so many shots are wide that it is suggested a group of three be arranged with one as the goalkeeper, with a shooter on either side of the goal. Each shooter fields shots from the other side of the goal, and then allowing the goalkeeper time to rotate, then shoots from his own side. After ten shots the group rotate.

By increasing the group to five, the same system can be used for more advanced combined dribbling, passing and shooting practice.

F. Heading (Upper Juniors only)

This particular skill, if practised too soon with a heavy ball, loses its entire value, since the natural tendency to self-preservation supersedes all other motives. It is best commenced as fun, with a light 5½-in. or 7½-in. playball.

- (a) There is much to recommend the practice of each boy holding the ball at forehead height, and continually heading it out of his own hands with his forehead.
- (b) Hand feeding for correct heading in twos or threes.
- (c) Heading for distance from hand feed.
- (d) Heading for direction from hand feed.
- (e) Combined with goalkeeper and feeder – heading for goal.
- (f) HEADING CRICKET – full details on a separate page.

G. Throwing In

- (a) Correct stance and throw – individual.
- (b) Throwing for direction – pairs, threes, combined with stopping, trapping, passing.
- (c) Throwing combined with returned heading.
- (d) Throwing for distance.

Kicking Cricket

Two sets of cricket stumps or boxes can be used. Teacher bowls by hand from one end only. Whenever the ball is kicked the batsmen must run – all runs are valid.

Ways to be out:

1. Any fielder who gets his head, chest or foot to the ball before it hits the ground dismisses a batsman caught.
2. Any fielder may trap and kick the ball to hit either wicket; if the kicker is not in his ground he is run out.
3. Any fielder who heads the ball three times dismisses the whole of the kicking team.

Penalties against fielders: any fielder touching the ball with his hands gives the kicking team six runs.

A size 3 or 4 Frido ball is recommended for this game.

Heading Cricket

Rules and penalties exactly as for kicking cricket – teacher feeds the ball to be headed by batsman.

Framework of Organized Games Lesson

All physical skills are acquired by practice and application to realistic situations, consequently in earlier years the simple enjoyable skills practised in the early part of the lesson can be made into simple games or relays to complete the lesson. As children grow, the more directed practices either class or group must be finally tested and improved in situations which are realistic to their stage of development. On this basis it is recommended that any organized games lesson should be divided so that one-third is devoted to skill training; and the remaining two-thirds to playing some form of the full game.

To make the lesson worth while, i.e. economic use of time, space and the creation of an enjoyable atmosphere, planning is needed. The essential qualities required from the teacher are INTEREST and ENTHUSIASM, with personal expertise a secondary consideration. If the pattern of changing clothes, establishing groups, and availability of equipment is 'grooved in', and you expect a good standard, encouraging all to improve, great pleasure and improved skill will result in even the most unfavourable physical situations.

Shinty and Hockey

During the Infant and Lower Junior years children have the opportunity to use sticks of varying shapes and sizes to acquire the skill of hitting a ball. For many this is a satisfying experience since in some ways it is an easier skill than trying to hit a bouncing ball or bobbing shuttle, and they are quite happy with this challenge. Later, however, the skill must be used in a purposeful way in order to stimulate interest and greater efforts to refine and expand this ability.

Due to apparatus availability in the past this need has been answered by introducing shinty (an informal type of hockey) into the programme. Since this has proved to be a successful game in its own right, which many schools will continue to play, it seems logical to present both shinty and hockey together.

In recent years hockey sticks suitable in size and weight for Juniors have come on to the market, and in the later stages of Junior school life;

certainly in Middle school days, progression from shinty towards hockey is desirable.

Both games need a good level surface if they are to be successful and are often therefore played on hard surface areas such as playgrounds or asphalt tennis courts. Hockey and particularly shinty balls can be terrifying to beginners on such a surface, leading to the recommendation that a soft-core ball approximating in weight to a hockey ball be used in these circumstances. If grass is preferred or is the only available facility, play when it is short and the ground dry, i.e. in the summer.

Apparatus

Shinty sticks: 5s to 8s each

Hockey sticks:

   28 in., 12–15 oz. – 15s to 17s 6d each.

   30 in., – 20s each (approx.)

Hockey shapes – 5s to 7s each

Shinty balls: 3s to 4s 6d each

Hockey balls:

   Composition – 4s 6d each

   Rubber cover – 9s 6d each

   Soft core – 9s 5d each

Goals

Ash staves or corner flags serve this purpose.

Pads

Soccer pads for players, football boots and small cricket pads for goalkeeper.

Portable Storage

A very useful portable storage trolley suitable for both shinty and hockey equipment can be made from 'lost' or redundant dinner trolleys of the wooden tray double tier type. By either boring individual holes or cutting out rectangles in the top tray all the sticks can be stored and transported at once, avoiding a mêlée in the apparatus store doorway. Bibs, posts and balls can be stored on the lower shelf between the handles of the sticks. Such trolleys designed to accommodate equipment for cricket, hockey, shinty and tennis may be purchased at a cost of £15 to £18. *Costs:* equipment costs vary from area to area, and from time to time. Many of the items quoted here can be purchased at lower figures under block purchase schemes operated by many authorities, and through local traders with whom the school has 'invisible links'; therefore it is possible to equip for shinty and hockey without massive expenditure. Two dozen sticks, half a dozen good balls supplemented by old rounders balls or tennis balls and an amended school meals trolley is all that is needed.

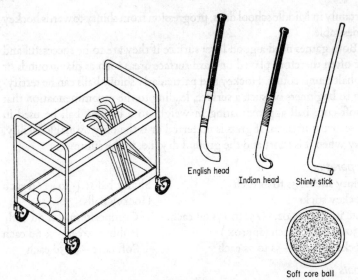

English head

Indian head

Shinty stick

Soft core ball

Starting the Game, i.e. either Shinty or Hockey

Two essentials should be stressed over and over again from the very beginning, namely the correct order of hands on the stick, i.e. left hand above right, and most important of all the avoidance of wild stick swinging. The personal danger involved may well be a more persuasive approach than any undue stress on the illegality of the practice. If this stick control is not firmly implanted, very little 'learning' will be possible and the whole point and enjoyment of the game will be lost.

Practices: using shinty or hockey shapes as available.

A. Dribbling
  1. Dribbling at slow speed across space turning right at each end, keeping ball close.
  2. Same practice gradually increasing speed as control develops.
  3. 'Scoring runs', most successful trips in 30 seconds, or minute.
  4. Free dribbling, keeping ball within a foot of the stick and avoiding other children.
  5. Increase difficulty of 4, by adding controlled speed, stopping, starting.
  6. Stationary ball, run, stick close to ground, take ball on into dribble.
  7. Dribbling, controlled hit ahead, catch up, dribble on, turn right and repeat stressing the necessity of concentrating on ball.

8. Pairs or threes with bean bags, blocks or skittles, create group obstacle course changing arrangement from time to time and dribble round course. Stress variation of spacing and use of zigzag and circle patterns.
9. Relays based on dribbling, e.g. round one skittle turn right and return, in and out of several skittles, using many small teams to increase activity.

B. Tackling

1. Pairs slowly: dribble combined with tackle from front, blocks for goals can be added to encourage tackling back and dribbling if successful in tackle.
2. Two against two, small game development in restricted area to encourage tackling and dribbling, no hitting allowed, tackling from front, open side and rear only.
3. Pairs: trying to tackle on dribbler's left; difficulty may prove too great in which case discourage, there will be time to add this skill when they are more mature.

C. Rolling

1. Rolling ball in pairs: stick in free hand, bend both knees and roll in varying directions along ground to partner who stops ball and rolls back.
2. Pairs: roll, stop using stick and push back to partner.
3. Threes: roll, stop or push to third player, rotate positions.

D. Pushing and Hitting

1. Pairs 10 yds apart, pushing ball backwards and forwards, aiming for controlled hit and immediate return, gradually increasing distance within reasonable limits.
2. Pairs: using wall or solid fence. Push or hit at an angle to rebound ball from surface to partner who can either stop, steady or immediately hit return pass. Regular changing of positions will ensure practice of stopping and hitting from both sides.
3. Threes: push ball ahead, run and overtake the ball, turn right, stop or steady the ball and push ball back to next player; with three, continuous practice is possible. Relays can be created using dribbling, stopping, pushing and hitting to ensure that a truer idea of 'game speed' in an enjoyable manner may be presented.

E. Passing and Shooting

1. Pairs passing across space being used: slowly increasing distance, emphasize aiming to hit ball into partner's running area, aiming eventually that neither partner needs to stop running, and the ball does not stop moving.
2. Threes rotating places, allowing enough running space for centre player to practise at least two passes to left and two to right.
3. Fours: include small goal and goalkeeper, passing and shooting. Goalkeeper can stop shot by hand, foot or stick rolling it out for repeat practice.

Pairs (practise 'bully') when proficient can create little competitions such as best of five bullies, or bully, dribble shoot at skittle or wall mark.

Small group games can be included from earliest stages by having 2 against 2, or 3 against 3 in defined areas using skills practised at time. Emphasis on passing can be made by ensuring that each player in the team must have touched the ball before a goal may be scored.

Gradually build these essential small-side games up to six-or seven-a-side, incorporating features you wish to stress, e.g. hit out by goalkeeper, corner, penalty corner, off-side. It may well be that you do not wish to include these particular features, and prefer to work on much simpler lines with children of this age.

Where space is limited, e.g. smaller playground or netball court the following methods may prove useful:

Change Hockey or Shinty

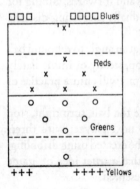

Example: Class of 28, divided into 4 teams of 7, each team wearing braids, Reds, Blues, Yellows and Greens. Goals made by bean bags, suitable chalk marks for shooting areas. Reds and Blues go to one end of court and Yellows and Greens to other end. Reds play Greens, other teams being part of game although off the court. On command change, Reds are immediately replaced by Blues and Greens by Yellows. Any two colours at opposing ends may be called, everyone should be alert waiting for their turn.

Six-or Five-a-side Games

These can also be played on 'Change Hockey' lines – quickly switching teams from one court to another to meet new opponents. The only guide needed for when to call 'Change' is one's acquired personal experience.

In the wider space required to have such groupings, friendly interest can be added by arranging an 'all play all' tournament, having a series of short games with minimum rules using the 'walking wounded' as timekeepers and recorders. Explanation of plan and particularly of rotation to be used beforehand is well worth while.

Shinty: Area and Rules

Area: adjustable according to space available – guide for Junior groups 7- to 11-a-side would be 30 to 50 yds wide and 45 to 70 yds long. There must be enough space to prevent crowding and to allow reasonable hitting.

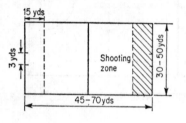

Shooting area may be made into circle if preferred. As shown shots at goal may be taken from anywhere within 15-yd limit.

Game started with centre bully or hit-off.

Balls passing over side or end lines can be 'hit on' or 'rolled-on' by any member of non-offending side; all other players being 3–5 yds away.

All fouls – free hit from spot – others 3–5 yds away.

A simple, speedy game should be the aim, introducing if desired the hockey corner, and a form of off-side rule which requires all hits by attackers in 15-yd area, other than shots at goal to be in a backward direction.

Strict enforcement of rules prohibiting 'sticks', i.e. stick above shoulder height at front or rear, kicking, rough play and obstruction will slowly ensure that the game you are striving to teach will eventually appear.

The same game can be played using 'hockey shapes' which are often preferred by juniors since they have a wider and truer hitting area. If these weapons are used they should also be employed in the skill practices. Although this is a simple game it still requires a period of deliberate and graduated skill practice each lesson, before battle commences.

Junior Hockey

Field or hard area marked out as in diagram suitable for teams of seven or eight players on each team. Adjustments in area can be made to accommodate larger teams, but teams of seven are recommended wherever possible.

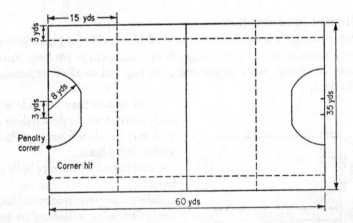

Rules

1. Game is started, restarted after half-time, and after goals by bully at centre. The sticks of each player must touch the ground and each other three times before ball is struck by either player. All other players should be within their own half and at least 5 yds from the ball.

2. Ball must be hit from within the circle and pass over the line to score.

3. Players are forbidden to:
   (a) raise stick above shoulder level (front or rear)
   (b) use back of stick
   (c) strike or hook opponent's stick
   (d) obstruct in any way
   (e) kick the ball, i.e. except goalkeeper

All such offences merit a free hit to the non-offending side from place of infringement. Other players at least 5 yds away from striker.

4. Ball passing over side line is returned to play by 'roll-in', taken by any member of non-offending side having feet and stick outside the line. The ball may be rolled in any direction, all other players being beyond the 3-yd line.

5. If attacking team send ball over goal line without scoring, the game is restarted by free hit taken 8 yds from goal line opposite place where it went out of play.

6. Corner – taken from corner hit position. Four defenders behind own goal line, rest beyond 15-yd line. Attackers outside circle – none within 5 yds of ball. Ball must be stopped before shot is taken.

7. Penalty corner – given when defender deliberately hits ball over own goal line. Same procedure as for corner, using penalty corner hit spot on either side of goal.

8. Breach of rules – outside circle free hit to other side; inside circle – defenders' offence – attackers gain penalty corner; inside circle – attackers offend – defenders awarded free hit which may be taken from any spot in the circle.

Rugby

It may come as a surprise to some teachers to find this game included here. In some areas, however, rugby of one code or another has been played by top juniors for many years, reflecting the adult interest and follow-up potential in Secondary school and later life.

Played in its full sense there can be little doubt that it has no part to play in Junior school games planning, but presented on a small-side basis substituting 'touching' for tackling it can provide an enjoyable acquaintance with a group of 'handling and kicking skills' with an odd-shaped ball. Many boys who have not mastered the foot controls of soccer are particularly grateful to try a game such as 'touch rugby', and even the expert soccer players often enjoy a change towards the end of a long season.

The skills of running, passing, fielding, catching, kicking, swerving and dodging practised singly, combined, and in the form of relays, followed by simple small-side games of the 'touch' type will therefore be the limits suggested here. With such experience behind them the boys will be able to face the fuller rigours of the game in later stages with more confidence, and possibly discover the 'enjoyment' which is certainly present when rugby is well taught.

Apparatus

Rugby balls: plastic, moulded rugby balls, sizes 3 and 4 – 6s to 10s each. Moulded rubber – £2 to £3 each – unnecessary at this stage.

Clothing: as for soccer.

Posts: cricket stumps, ash staves, stationary boys when required.

Fundamentals

There is a peculiar fascination buried somewhere inside an oval ball, when all your previous experience has been acquired with round balls of differing sizes but fairly predictable behaviour patterns. Given the space, and enough plastic rugby balls for one to three or four, let them try throwing it, kicking it and picking it up for some time before introducing any particular skill training.

'Little and often' skill training, with the object of keeping everybody busy immediately before 'adapted' game should then be the method to follow.

Practices—Running, Swerving and Dodging

Using ball, these activities can be practised together in relay forms using teams of three for individual type relays, and teams of four for shuttle type:

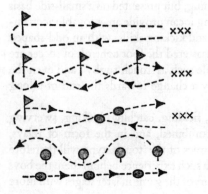

1. Run, turn round mark (skittle, bean bag, cane) set 10 to 15 yds away, return, give ball to next in team. Whole team four to six times.

2. Same arrangement using obstacles – swerve and dodge, 'give' ball to next runner.

3. As number 1 'pass' ball to next runner.

4. As number 2 'pass' ball to next runner.

5. Same formation – run, 'place' ball, i.e. score on outward trip, pick it up on run and pass to next runner.
6. Run, score at turning point, leaving ball, touch next runner off who returns with ball 'passing' it in.
7. Team spread 4 to 5 yds apart standing ready to pass, ball quickly passed to rear runner who dodges in and out of team members to front.

These relays and many others of this type may be repeated in shuttle, wheel or circular formation as shown in diagram if preferred.

Shuttle Formation
Distance apart can be varied – watch change-overs.

Circle Formation

Wheel Formation
Ball passed along from centre to outside.

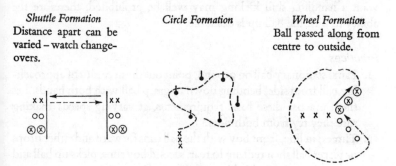

Passing

In the earliest stages 'wild, hopeful throws' in any direction may well be the order of the day. Deliberate passing practices are therefore essential, originally merely to project the ball to an intended team-mate, and gradually including the basic essential of passing backwards.

Stressing the features of 'looking – swinging the arms across the body – and trying to pass waist high in front of receiver' will suffice in most cases. Keen rugby teachers may well go much further than this, but all should be guided at this stage by the effectiveness rather than the style of the action.

Practices

1. Pairs: throwing and catching briefly, turning sideways 'passing' either standing or walking. Use 'natural' pair to demonstrate.
2. Pairs: same activity at 'trot', later 'run', turning at set place to gain experience of passing from either side.

3. Pairs: one standing ready to pass to partner as he runs past.
4. Threes: passing on run at controlled speed, changing middle man frequently.
5. Fours: 2 against 2, successful passes counted, restrict area, add dodging and touch.
6. Fives: 3 against 2, touch and pass, timing element, threes should score.

Fielding Ball
At first the ball may well be on the ground a great deal and since you want a handling skill kicking may well be prohibited, therefore the ability to pick the ball up is desirable.

Practices
1. Pairs: stationary ball on ground, point out the necessity of approaching ball from side, bending down to grasp ball with both hands. Let them practise these basic requirements, at varying speeds making sure they try from both sides.
2. Threes: in line, front boy with the ball runs forward and either drops or places ball then retiring to rear, second boy runs, picks up ball and repeats process for third boy – self repeating activity.
3. Pairs: stand facing 5 or 6 yds apart, rolling ball, fielding and rolling back, gradually rolling to either side, constant speed fielding and movement.
4. Pairs: roll ball past fielder who turns, fields and passes back.
5. Pairs: farther apart, low throws to pitch short and bounce awkwardly in front and later to side, repeated.
6. Pairs: 5 to 6 yds apart, feet wide apart, throw or roll at speed to try to score by getting the ball through partner's legs.

Kicking and Catching
Although obviously allied, initial difficulties occur in both these skills which make it easier to separate their introductory stages.

Kicking
It is often profitable to go through the actions of the basic punt kick without the ball, emphasizing that the ball is held in both hands and

almost placed on the instep as the kicking leg swings through, otherwise the type of one handed toss in the air will appear with which they are familiar.

Practices

1. Class: dummy punt action without the ball, both hands, head down, place ball, kick and follow through.
2. Pairs: ball, punt and field, catch if possible.
3. Pairs: trying to kick accurately to partner who in earliest stages fields; later, having had catching practice, tries to catch.
4. Pairs: punting with the 'other' foot.
5. Pairs: kicking for distance – insist on punt if teaching that particular kick.

Place Kicking

A compulsive activity and one which can keep boys happily engaged whilst late changers arrive. Posts can be created by kicker by using canes, having partner stand arms raised to give crossbar height.

Simplest method should be shown, viz: reasonable heel mark, 'place ball upright', i.e. balance it, do not push or screw it in, step back, run up and try to lift ball off the ground by toe kicking at base of ball, over-emphasizing the strong upward follow through. Early attempts should be within easy range preferably from immediately in front of 'post'. The placing of the non-kicking foot alongside the ball and the follow through will need repeating.

Catching

As in all forms of catching the 'watch the ball' element must be stressed, particularly in this case since opponents approach at considerable speed with the sole object of spoiling your endeavours. Due to the shape of the ball it must be pointed out that it is much easier to run forward to make the catch, and to catch the ball before it bounces. The main points to be stressed will be to make a 'cradle' with the arms bent, fingers spread, elbows in, bringing the ball into the chest where it can be firmly grasped.

Practices

1. Class: quickly practise the 'action' of catching described.

2. Pairs: feeder throwing short high ball to be caught and fed back. Good deliberate feeding is essential.
3. Pairs: feeder throwing high so that partner has to move forward to make catch.
4. Pairs: increase range and direction of feeding.
5. Pairs: add practice punting and catching.

Game Form of Kicking and Catching
Gaining Ground
Two, three, maximum four a side – define area according to local conditions, e.g. useful to use lines of existing pitches playing across marked pitch.

Goals if required – cricket stumps, canes – not really necessary.

Rules
Team A kick off from area indicated in diagram. Any type of kick, preferably a punt.

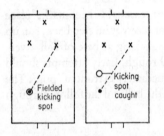

Opponents stop, field or catch the ball as soon as they are able. If stopped or fielded, quickly step back and then run up to spot where ball was stopped and kick ball back. Object: to try to kick the ball beyond opponents or deep into areas not well defended, i.e. gain ground.

Kicks caught on full allowed to take three running strides forward and then kick, or to take place kick at goal. Opposition form uprights – if passes between posts above ground scores 3 points.

This simple game is capable of numerous interpretations, and if presented frequently is capable of developing kicking, catching and 'insight' tactical skill.

Touch Rugby
After the early skill training period the simplest form of this type of rugby should be played with small groups of 6 or 7 a side to round off the lesson. As time passes and confidence and control grow the rules of the game to follow can be amended to stress the skills previously practised. Three

stages of growth are suggested but many individual rules can be incorporated to suit particular requirements.

Apparatus
Size 4 rugby ball, 'bibs' for at least one team, ash staves, if goals desired.

Space
Rectangular area approximately 60 yds by 40 yds – basic outside lines.

First Stage
1. Start free pass from centre – restart after scoring in same way.
2. Run in any direction carrying ball until 'touched' by opponent, must then pass; the pass must be made quickly but can be in any direction.
3. Score by grounding the ball over opponents' goal line without having been touched.
4. Rough play, ball out of play and any other emergencies: free pass to opposition.
5. The ball may not be kicked or punched or even stolen from opponents.

Second Stage
Add line 10 yds from each goal line, and 'vague' positions.
1. Start and operate rules as before adding one stipulation:
2. Passes in opponents' 10-yd area must be backwards; free pass to other team from 'forward pass' position added to penalties.

Third Stage
Capable of many personal additions according to ability of players. Same game ALL passes must be BACKWARD. Additions possible:
1. Place kicks for goal after scoring.
2. Kicking: punts in defence, grubbers, i.e. kicks along ground in attack.

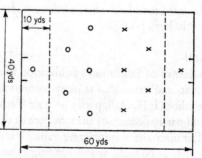

3. Small line-outs: positions appear.
4. Three-boy scrums: positions appear.
5. Touch and play: when touched must stop and either pass or heel ball through legs to a team-mate. One opponent stands in front of 'heeler', remainder retire 5 yds.
6. Four touch: after four touches without scoring the ball is given to the other team.

Many of these additions prove useful in the earliest stages of Secondary or Middle school life and indeed are often used either in this form or substituting tackling for touching for team training at a variety of stages including adult level.

Sometimes a group express a desire to 'try' tackling – usually the biggest and strongest show most interest. If you are unsure about this aspect firmly omit it from your scheme. If, however, this is within your experience and you know the boys better than many of them know themselves, some experience of mass murder similar to many playground scenes can be incorporated by having a game of Tackling Tag. This is simply two or three original tacklers past whom the remainder have continually to run from one safe area to another. Those tackled join the tacklers, the winner being the last man untackled.

If during the course of their last two years in the Junior school the boys learn to catch, kick and pass an oval ball and can use these skills adequately even to the second stage suggested here they will have had a valuable experience on which to build. This idea of giving juniors a taste of several differing skills will become increasingly important as more and more Middle and Secondary schools offer a wider variety of games than has previously been possible.

Netball
The Ministry of Education's publication *Planning the Programme* states: 'The National game that is most commonly played at the top of the Junior school is Netball, partly because Netball courts are usually available and partly because of the influence of the Secondary schools where netball is often the major winter game. It is open to question whether a game such as Netball, where running must be severely checked, is an appropriate game for children at a stage when it is their habit to run

rather than walk. Generally speaking, juniors will enjoy the national games most when they play their own version of them. Sides should be smaller than is customary and the fewest possible rules should be introduced.'

In 1963 the All England Netball Association published the first edition of their excellent booklet *An Introduction to Netball in Junior Schools* giving a wealth of information about the game of 'Junior Netball'. It is towards this game rather than its adult form which juniors should be coached.

Despite the sound caution about stopping when in possession pointed out in Planning the Programme, with good coaching junior children are capable of playing this game very well and with great enthusiasm. Boys particularly gain greatly in appreciation for other games by occasionally playing a game in which they are obliged to stop and look before parting with the ball. For this reason (although netball is widely regarded as the girls' province), more 'mixed' games might prove beneficial.

Whilst aiming towards junior netball two other games using the same basic rules, namely, free netball and skittleball played by either single sex or mixed groups, have often proved both useful and enjoyable as steps on the way. Consequently the details of these games will be included in this section, so that during a games lesson all three games might be operating simultaneously, offering sufficient scope for all abilities.

Equipment
Posts and Stands
These may be purchased from many firms, costs varying between £12 to £15 per pair. Junior schools must make sure that the stands they buy are adjustable, so that the net may be fixed at heights varying between 8 and 10 ft. The other important feature to note is the shape of the stand itself. There are a variety of shapes available (as shown in diagram), but since in junior netball the stand is placed 3 ft inside the court it is strongly recommended that a circular cast-iron form of stand be purchased.

Many schools may prefer to make their own stands and purchase only brackets and rings, or indeed to dispense with stands entirely using wall fixings either for practice purposes or where space is restricted for full games. Rings alone may cost approximately 30s a pair, and the brackets about 7s a pair. If possible it is well worth having nets fixed to the rings since it is so much easier to judge when a goal is scored – such nets will cost in the region of 9s to 10s per pair.

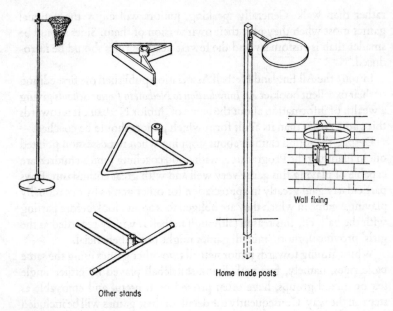

Wall fixing

Home made posts

Other stands

Netballs

For general use and practice: plastic Frido, size 4 – 8s to 9s each. If preferred regulation plastic, size 4 – 11s each.

For matches, rallies and team practice two or three moulded rubber balls reserved for the purpose should be available costing between £2 to £3 each.

Since most schools have a supply of the heavy Frido balls which can be used for numerous games this is usually a relatively inexpensive game to mount in a school, especially when local funds are available to assist with the purchase of posts.

Main Skills

A. Footwork: ability to run, stop, dodge and swerve quickly in order to get free and mark.
B. Ball handling: to propel and receive ball with control and accuracy.
C. Combination of A and B: essential for success and progress.
D. Defensive play and intercepting.
E. Shooting: the whole point of the game.

Practices

All practices are in progressive order and a good lesson can be planned by taking one or two practices from each group and adding a game of some related form as a concluding feature. To achieve very good results it is important to really master the earlier stages before moving on to more difficult practices.

A. Footwork

1. Individually: running with sudden change of pace – sudden stop on whistle signal.
2. Individually: running with sudden change of direction, sudden stops on signal.
3. Combination of 1 and 2 including stopping: jumping high in air on signal.
4. As 3 but with opponent: one dodging, the other marking, trying to avoid opponent by using changes of pace, direction, and sudden stops.
5. Individually dodging in a *confined* space: emphasizing side to side movement (avoid dancing steps), short vigorous steps with slightly bent knees.
6. 'Shadows': as in 5 but with opponent – accent on dodging. This practice is particularly valuable for shooters and situations where marking is tight.
7. As 6: accent on marking, no facing opponent.
8. Game forms of these activities: emphasizing dodging much more than running and chasing.

   (a) *One Against Three:* three children join hands to form triangle, fourth child attempts to touch child farthest away. Changing frequently.

   (b) *Whistle Race:* children race across space; each time whistle blows they turn about and race in the opposite direction.

   (c) *Fox and Geese:* three children line up behind each other holding the waist of the child in front. The fourth, the fox, stands facing them and at a signal tries to touch the goose's tail. Later front child can stretch out his arms to make task more difficult.

   (d) *Chinese Wall:* parallel lines 10 ft apart are drawn to represent the wall across centre of space. Three or four children defend the

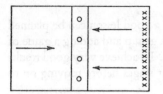

wall, remainder try to cross wall without being touched by defenders. When touched either join defenders or continue running counting how many times touched on six trips through.

These practices form the basic skill of netball footwork and need intensive training and frequent revision even when the game has been played for some time.

B. Ball Handling

Main Coaching Points: try to pass to 'unmarked' players of your own team if possible passing ahead of the player using whole body into the throw and varying the throw and force used according to partners distance and position of opposition.

When catching watch the ball, move into its path and try to use both hands, springing up to catch high passes and letting the arms 'give' towards the side of the body from which one throws when the catch has been made.

Types of Throw

Shoulder throw: push ball with the hand behind it straight, hard, long.

Chest throw: push ball from chest with both hands, flick wrists – straight, short.

Overhead throw: push ball from above head with both hands – short, direct.

Underarm throw: shovel ball in any direction with both hands – short, low.

Using Frido 16-oz., size 4, footballs size 4 or large rubber balls – aim for one between two.

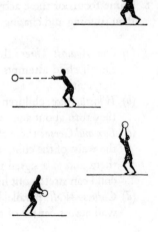

1. Shoulder throw in twos, threes or fours according to large balls available.
2. Chest throw in pairs.
3. Overhead throw in pairs, quickly changing to threes to 'pig in the middle'.
4. In twos, threes and fours on the move in defined area practising all the different methods of throwing, varying the distance of the passes. Catching can be stressed by counting number of successful passes achieved before ball is dropped.
5. Threes: middle player holds small hoop at knee, waist, chest and overhead levels – others pass through hoop using pass appropriate to height.
6. Jumping to catching high ball in twos, threes or fours: to teach jumping for high pass – the ball being thrown directly over receiver's head; they must learn to gauge their spring and reach for it with both hands.
7. One feeder facing two or three receivers who stand 10 to 12 yds away. In turn the receivers run forward, catch whichever type of pass the feeder decides to give them and return the ball to feeder. This is an advanced practice demanding skill and co-operation.

C. Combinations of Footwork and Ball Handling

Restrictions on footwork in junior netball are much less stringent than in the full game, and one ignores the step or two taken whilst catching on the run, nevertheless deliberate stepping must be penalized since if allowed the whole nature of the game is altered.

1. Pairs: RUNNING (not slip step sideways), about 8 ft apart – passing. Check the number of steps taken before parting with the ball aiming to reduce gradually this number. Overemphasize FORWARD RUNNING MOVEMENT.
2. Pairs: as number 1 but emphasizing passing ahead of partner and high so that partner has to jump to receive the ball.
3. Progress to include three or four players all moving up the court.
4. 'Keep the ball moving': using wall as goal and including shot. Start in loose group, insist on forward passes, start again if ball is dropped.

Game forms are particularly useful and enjoyable for this stage, examples being:

1. Circle pass out: children pair off and form circle with one partner standing in front of the other. In the earliest stages the teacher is in the middle of the circle with the ball, but should be replaced by child as soon as competence permits. Outer ring are in fact a team to whom the centre player is trying to pass the ball. Inner ring defenders try to intercept the ball. When interception takes place ball is returned to centre, game continues. Great emphasis on 'getting free' by dodging and passing to free side of player insisting on shoulder or underarm throws. Incentive can be added by scoring, calling out score as pass is made, each team having 3 to 5 minutes.

This excellent practice needs constant revision and can be taken with the emphasis on attack or defence, in groups of five, seven, etc., or with one-quarter or even half the class as a group activity. Children must be able to dodge and pass adequately before using a 'central' child.

2. Numbered passing in fours: helps to see quickly free player and to pass accurately to him. Number 1 starts with the ball, the other three in a moving group close to him, calls for number 2 who signals with his hand exactly where he wants it, receives it correctly and passes before third step to number 3 whom he has called and so on.
3. Dodge ball in threes: i.e. middle player dodging to avoid being hit below knee by ball.
4. Intercepting in threes: i.e. middle player trying to intercept passes.
5. Two against two: game of numbered continuous successful passes.
6. Three against two: change attack and defence to show advantage of extra person.
7. Three against three: one-way goal. Both teams observing major rules try at the same time to score and prevent other side scoring in the same goal. Wall brackets are extremely useful for such 'mini-games'.

D. Defensive Play and Intercepting

Although these skills are inseparable from many of the previous practices there is often a need to draw special attention to them in their own right.

1. Fours, threes or even pairs: 'snatching' the loose ball off the ground.

Practice of this rather 'unsocial' skill often sharpens the children's reaction to seeing the ball on the ground, to gaining possession and preventing a tug of war. The ball should be seen, snatched and pulled into the throwing position before years of social training to do exactly the opposite have time to intervene.

2. Deliberate intercepting in threes: i.e. defence player *marking* opponent only, avoiding overhead throw. This teaches accurate passes to player's free side.

3. Fours – three jumpers and thrower: ball is thrown up vertically, three jumpers must judge their spring and try to get to the ball with arms outstretched as when jumping for misshot under goal-ring.

4. Wandering ball: circle with four or five players round perimeter, two less within. Ball is passed across circle quickly, varying height and direction of pass. Feints should be made to deceive interceptors. Any interception means thrower takes interceptor's place within.

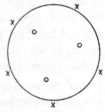

E. Shooting

Intention, action and decision of success or failure are so immediate, and some measure of success so vital in the early stages that low attainable goals at 8 ft are recommended. It is easy and logical to raise this to 8 ft 6 in. if it is too easy, adding a new target, but far more difficult to lower with success if constant failure has been encountered. They may indeed still be capable but may also have lost interest which may be difficult to recapture.

1. Coach shooting technique: face goal, one foot forward, bend knees and push the ball upwards and forwards, aiming for a high curve into the net. Emphasize economy of time over preparation, finding own personal style and following up shots that miss.

   Much valuable practice can take place if rings and netballs are available with a little reserved space during breaks and particularly at midday.

2. Twos: turns to shoot from different marked positions, varied distances. Partner fields, returns ball and then has equivalent number of shots from same positions. Can be made competitive.

3. Twos: pass from player in circle, taken by partner running into circle, shot taken, places changed – capable of many variations of position, speed and type of pass.
4. Threes: player outside circle with ball, attacker and defender within. After successful pass, shot taken – players rotate functions.
5. Free shooting in teams against time limit: no player is allowed consecutive shots, so that all get equal chances.
6. Shooting practice in fours: each player has three consecutive shots, the other three players jump under the post and try to keep the ball in play.

Lines of Progress

First phase: vigorous directed period of training whole class in footwork and ball handling, particularly using small group activities, e.g. team passing in pairs as game element. Basic units of six should be built in, enabling pairs, threes and a small team to be readily available.

Second phase: shorten introductory section, slowly include all skills sections and conclude lesson using small areas for, e.g. 10 skittleball, 10 free netball, and 10 netball changing so that the teacher can build up proficiency by coaching 10 in turn at the latter activity.

Alternative: after short introductory and class skills, class is divided into three groups as follows: (i) 10 – both netball rings – shooting – total score of group in 5 minutes, (ii) 10 – teacher – circle pass out – passes in 5 minutes, (iii) 10 – one-way goal using skittle or skittleball – score in 5 minutes.

The activities can be made progressively more difficult if desired.

Third phase: emphasis on selected class skills increasing speed followed by: (i) 10 playing free netball, (ii) 10 playing skittleball, (iii) 10 playing netball – changing from group to group should be within same lesson but due to shortage of time might possibly be on weekly rota basis. Older children who are 'walking wounded' can be used to umpire two of the games if such officials are required.

Final phase: selective skill training, followed by two games of junior netball. where Middle schools exist or are planned this phase might well be included in the early stages of their progress to the full game.

The diagrams which are included to illustrate the suggested arrangements for the alternative second phase, the third phase, and the basic rules of the three games mentioned are based on the availability of a playground space approximately 100 ft × 50 ft for 30 children.

Both possibilities diagrammatically represented, using one-third of netball court for each group using length of court to full advantage.

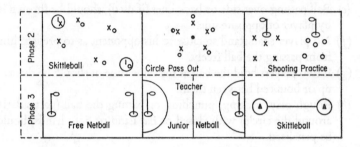

Skittleball

Length of line – 40 to 70 ft. Circle – 7 to 8 ft diameter. Number on each side – 5, 7 (usual) or any odd number of players.

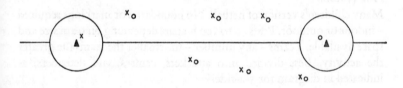

Game

The teams consists of an odd number of players; a skittle guard and an equal number of players (paired off with an opponent as per diagram) on each side of the line. If preferred the line may be omitted. The object is to knock down the opponents skittle with the ball – 2 points being scored in this way. If the skittle is knocked down by the guard 1 point is scored. Shots at the target can be made from any position, and players should move about trying to find an opening from which to take aim.

Rules

(a) Game is started by a bounce or throw up between two opposing players in the middle.

(*b*) No player may run with the ball or hold it for more than three seconds.

(*c*) No player may cross the centre line (when used), nor enter the circles.

(*d*) Skittle guard may come out of circle.

(*e*) Ball passing over side or back lines (if used), should be thrown in by player of opposite side.

(*f*) No player shall stand so close to his opponent as to prevent him from passing the ball freely.

(*g*) If two players hold the ball at the same time, it should be thrown up or bounced between them.

(*h*) Rough play, kicking, punching or batting the ball (particularly around the circle) with closed or flat hand or both hands should be penalized.

PENALTY FOR INFRINGEMENT OF RULES: FREE THROW TAKEN ON THE SPOT

Free Netball

Many children's version of netball. No boundaries or markings required – indoor or outdoor. Posts 50 to 100 ft apart depending on team size and space available. Teams – any number – the smaller the teams the greater the activity. Best divided into attackers, centres, and defenders, as indicated in diagram for 5-a-side.

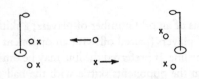

Method of Play

1. Start with centre pass. Restart after each goal in same way.
2. Ball may be passed in any direction with one or both hands.
3. Anyone may score from any position – unobstructed shot.
4. Stop when in possession – pass or shoot as soon as possible.

Scoring: one point per goal.

Fouls

1. Carrying ball.
2. Kicking, fisting or heading the ball.
3. Any form of rough play.
4. Knocking or pulling ball from opponent's hands.
5. Touching post during shot.

Penalties: free throw from place of infringement or 'sin bin'.

Coaching Points

1. Short, fast, accurate passing, using long 'hopeful' throws sparingly.
2. Dodging to get free to receive pass.
3. Shooting when within reasonable range, i.e. not too far away or underneath.
4. Play without shouting or argument.

Junior Netball

Court as shown desirable. Where reduced sizes used try to keep shooting circle as near full size as possible. Ring – 8, 9 or 10 ft as decided locally.

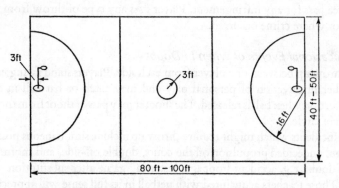

Seven players per team – 2 shooters, 2 defence and 3 centres who must be in appropriate court at pass off but are then free to move anywhere (except shooters and defence may not enter the circle at the far end). Centre players may not enter either circle.

Out and In: ball is out when it or player holding it touches ground outside court. Opposite side throw it in with feet behind line where ball crossed line. If uncertain of culprit take throw up in vicinity of occurrence. Off-side, i.e. centre player in circle – free throw from spot.

Main Rules

Players may catch ball in any manner, and may throw or bounce it in any direction to another player.

When in possession must pass or shoot within three seconds (liberally interpreted) and will be allowed to move feet on spot and where necessary take a step or two before parting with the ball.

Fouls

1. Rolling or kicking the ball.
2. Trying to take ball from opponent.
3. Throwing up, or bouncing the ball individually continuously.
4. Handing the ball to team-mate.
5. Trying to impede or intercept a shot for goal.
6. Rough play or obstruction.

Penalties Awarded

Free pass for any infringement. Player uses any type of throw from the spot where crime occurred.

Occasional Events or when in Doubt

Throw up between one player from each side. Players stand facing each other in direction of personal play and may catch or bat ball in any direction when ball is released. The shooter may pass or shoot from throw up in circle.

Incidents which might require throw up include simultaneous possession, undecided propulsion off the court, double off-side, and moments of doubt, e.g. accident stoppage, restarting game after substitution.

Those teachers acquainted with netball in its full sense will appreciate that the techniques and general form of this game are as for the full game with some of the more complicated rules omitted. To establish firmly the limits within which the children are able to operate it is suggested that umpiring, whilst being understanding in the earliest stages, should become more firmly applied with the passage of time and the increase of skill and tactical awareness. Without this proviso the game will not serve its intention of providing an excellent basis on which the children can progress in later years to the more exacting demands of the Secondary school.

Junior Basketball

A scaled-down version of basketball now exists, which has become very popular in those areas into which it has so far been introduced. The basic skills of running, jumping, bouncing, catching, throwing and dodging allied to simple rules in a no-contact constant action situation have great appeal to upper juniors.

Basic Rules MUST be observed whatever other local amendments may be made.

1. No contact.
2. One pace permitted carrying the ball.
3. One dribble, i.e. bouncing the ball with one hand or the other taking as many steps as preferred, when dribble ends ball must be passed to another player.

Such variation exists in the cost of stands that it would be unrealistic even to give approximate costs. In most cases they are the type of equipment with which a school would need some financial assistance from local sources. Existing netball stands might well be used initially but the backboard is such an essential feature of this game that their absence results in a mixture of basketball and netball.

Wall mounted netball rings are extremely useful for practice since the wall acts as a kind of backboard, and since ordinary size 5 heavy Frido's are used, much useful practice may be encouraged using such existing facilities.

Introducing the Game

Try to ensure that a size 4 or 5 heavy Frido ball is available for each three children taking part, and that a number of wall targets or rings at 8 ft 6 in. gradually appear. For the fuller games towards which you are aiming use the netball stands, making sure of course that they are not required for their designed purpose by a colleague.

Stages – stressing the simplicity of the game.

Court and Equipment

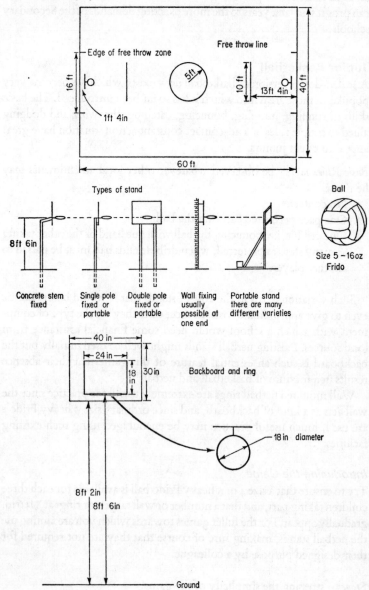

Edge of free throw zone

Free throw line

16 ft

1ft 4in

5ft

10 ft

13ft 4in

40 ft

60 ft

Types of stand

Ball

8ft 6in

Concrete stem fixed

Single pole fixed or portable

Double pole fixed or portable

Wall fixing usually possible at one end

Portable stand there are many different varieties

Size 5 – 16oz
Frido

40 in

24 in

18 in

30 in

Backboard and ring

18 in diameter

8ft 2in

8ft 6in

Ground

A. Passing

1. 2 *v*. I, game of Pig in the Middle, emphasizing short range, safe passing, with movement away from interceptor by receiver, and hand N O T verbal signals. From this simple game make the following points:

   (*a*) Always try to use both hands to pass and receive the ball.

   (*b*) Emphasize turning to face team-mate when you pass – feet in same direction as pass.

   (*c*) Hold ball steady with both hands in front of chest and under chin – avoid wild circling movements – thus instantly ready to pass when receiver runs free.

   (*d*) Deliberate pass into team-mate's running area by 'pushing' arms out and 'flicking' wrists.

   To allow this vital skill to be acquired have group practices in twos or threes, viz:

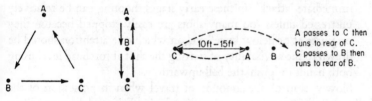

2. 2 *v*. I, pass fails and 'pig' is changed if:

   (*a*) ball is touched by interceptor

   (*b*) any loss of control by either passer or catcher

3. 2 *v*. 2, or 3 *v*. 3. Team passing, counting successful passes, if possible adding simple form of goal, e.g. netball ring, wall target. If goal is possible at one end of area only – 'one-way goal' game, i.e. must have at least three consecutive successful passes before shooting.

4. Introduce the pass to partner via the ground, aiming to keep ball low and 'skid' it to partner. Let them try 2 *v*. I.

5. Using similar arrangements as before practise this low pass emphasizing use of both, and either hand singly. Using 2 *v*. I, or 3 *v*. 2 groups encourage receivers running free, passer using 'direct' pass if possible, ground pass when closely guarded by larger opponent. All passes in range of 10 to 15 ft.

6. Passing from in front of shoulders should be stressed to avoid the

'soccer throw-in' pass which has little place in this situation. Unless a great deal of time is spent on eradicating this particular action and substituting a correct action allied to a jump if necessary, progress will be severely limited.

7. Having worked on the passes, feeding each back into small team games, encourage closer guarding without contact, 'feints' by passer to deceive the guard, keeping ball low, making 'deliberate' movements with the ball, always ready in passing position, and use of all kinds of passes. A pass is GOOD if it is deliberately delivered and arrives with certainty at its destination.

8. Passers should always be able to see team-mates and should try to face opponents' goal.

9. Each lesson MUST contain a good session of realistic 'play' based on skills taught, and in 3 *v*. 3, or 4 *v*. 4 games with targets, the emphasis should be placed on passing, running into space to receive the ball at short range, no contact but development of interception, and immediate 'attack'. In these early stages shooting can be relatively unstressed unless too many shots are easily stopped because they originate at or below knee level, in which case attention should be drawn to the advisability of starting the shot at forehead level using both hands to 'push' the ball upwards.

Slowly control the amount of travel when in possession of the ball – the all important aspect to aim for is efficient, deliberate, direct passing of the ball.

B. Shooting

1. Combining passing and shooting using goals or wall targets – 2 *v*. 1, or 3 *v*. 2 games – getting free by passing and moving and shooting, shooting and shooting again. Allow a reasonable time for groups to change round and observe types of shot used.

2. Deliberately teach fundamentals of 'lay-up' shot, if necessary without ball, viz, RUN, JUMP, REACH, then having done most of the work PUSH ball from one hand to score.

3. Groups using rings or targets: A runs in, shoots, collects rebound, passes to B, etc.

4. Bringing run down to three steps – stress JUMP, REACH and PUSH, pointing out three factors:
   (*a*) shooting hand should be behind ball

   (*b*) other hand steadies ball – is not operational at time of shot

   (*c*) jump off opposite foot to shooting hand, i.e. most cases left foot

   (*d*) ball pushed up straight in front of face, not round arm action

5. Group practice as previously – counting successful attempts out of ten or twenty.

6. To bring running within scope of essential rule – 'one pace with ball' – stand near target or ring, drop the ball, step collect ball, step and jump and shoot.

7. As skill develops it can be combined with passing and dribbling, adding realism by constantly returning to 2 *v.* 1, 3 *v.* 2, and team-passing games. Greatest practice can be achieved in free time if equipment is made available.

8. Set shots can be introduced and practised, particularly using free

Possible Group Practice Arrangements

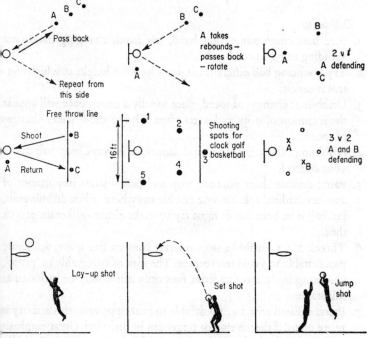

Run, jump, reach, push

throw line and by having certain designated spots from which to shoot and scoring how many set shots each boy needs to score from all of these spots.

9. Gradually an opponent can be included making the shooter 'feint' and then get his set shot in under pressure. At this stage some boys will jump to shoot naturally introducing the 'jump' shot. In both types of shot emphasize the following points:

  (a) face and look at target
  (b) control ball – hold in front of body with both hands at chin or forehead level, NOT below, bend knees and push upwards
  (c) balance yourself
  (d) flight ball with wrist and fingers
  (e) attempt only possible shots; if shot is doubtful, pass to a teammate to try to create a more favourable shooting position quickly.

Dribbling

1. Free bouncing: using right hand, left hand, changing hands but avoiding using BOTH hands.

2. Try bouncing ball different heights – look for height at which control is easiest.

3. Dribbling: changes of speed, since usually a group pace will appear the inclusion of stops and starts often helps to show wider changes of speed.

4. Dribbling: changing speed and direction. Always keep ball under your control.

5. Pairs: dribble short distance, stop and pass – stress importance of another cardinal rule, i.e. one dribble anywhere, when dribble ends, i.e. ball is in both hands must try to make either deliberate pass or shot.

6. Threes: 2 v. 1 – dribble, stop, receiver runs for free space, deliberate pass suitable to avoid interceptor. The idea of being able to 'pivot', i.e. swing body moving front foot only can slowly be included at this stage.

7. Pairs: defined area 1 v. 1 – dribble to beat opponent, this activity is more useful if shot at ring or target can be included. Great emphasis will need to be laid on role of potential interceptor now. Basically

the simplest way is to insist on NO CONTACT – a moving backward arms extended interception only role.

8. Groups of 3 *v*. 2, or 3 *v*. 3 on team passing and dribbling tasks including goals where possible.

9. Many forms of relay can be introduced using dribbling alone; dribbling combined with direct pass to next runner, dodging, dribbling and passing, and dribbling and shooting can profitably be included to put the skill under speed pressure in a mildly competitive manner.

10. Mass activities, e.g. maze of skittles, chairs, boxes – dribbling for avoidance, i.e. 'look where you are going not at the ball' can be used. Another form is to put all dribblers in confined area allowing them to disturb all other dribblers in any way without themselves losing control of their ball. Those disturbed beyond control drop out. This 'bull in the ring' activity is useful to repeat from time to time.

Although presented in the form of major skills at class activity level here, teachers may well prefer to have three or four groups working on different skills according to facilities available in the skill training section of their lesson, e.g. (i) team passing, (ii) lay-up shots, (iii) set shots, (iv) dribbling. In this way since each of the groups would rotate, a number of reinforcing skills would be acquired at the same time. A sound scheme might be gradually to move from class to group activities, sometimes including particular mass or relay activities and concluding each session with graded games according to the stage of ability reached.

Major Rules of Junior Basketball

Aim: to throw the ball into opponents' basket, after handling by throwing, passing or dribbling the ball in any direction within the court.

Teams and officials: five players constitute a team, playing for 15 minutes per half with 5-minute interval. A referee will control the game assisted by a timekeeper scorer responsible for these two important aspects of the game.

Scoring: one basket – two points; one basket from a free throw – one point.

Moving with the ball: a player who receives the ball whilst standing still may pivot on either foot. He may lift the pivot foot when he throws for goal or passes but the ball must leave his hands before he returns to earth. When a player comes to a stop with the ball, only the rear foot may be used as pivot foot. A player may not run carrying the ball. Penalty: free throw from side-line to opponents. A player may dribble the ball by hand, using one hand – never both – in any direction. When the ball comes to rest in one or both hands, he may not restart another dribble and must keep his rear foot at that moment still until he has passed the ball. Penalty: free throw from side-line to opponents.

Starting the game: 'jump ball', i.e. referee tosses ball up between two players. Each player may tap ball twice but may not catch it. Jump ball is awarded to start each half, when ball is held between two opponents, ball lodged in basket support, when ball is put out of play by two opponents. The ball is thrown up either in the centre circle or on free throw line nearest to the incident.

Personal fouls: a player may not hold, push, trip or charge an opponent nor use any rough tactics. Penalty: one foul recorded by scorer against culprit (5 fouls eliminate). Loss of ball if incident was accidental – free throw to opponents from side-line. Two free throws at basket if deliberate, or if the player fouled was shooting at the basket. If two players foul each other 'simultaneously' then a 'jump ball' results.

Technical fouls: award for unsporting conduct. Penalty: two free throws.

Free throw: allows unhindered throw at basket from behind free throw line, scoring one point if successful. Remaining players may occupy places outside free throw zone, two of the defenders in positions nearest the basket. No player may enter free throw zone before the ball touches the ring.

Penalties for infringements:
  by shooter – free throw to opponents from side line
  by defenders – scores one if successful, if not, another attempt allowed
  by team-mates of shooter – count if scored, otherwise free throw.

Ball out of play: when a player in possession of the ball touches boundary, side or end lines with any part of the body the ball is out of play. Similarly when the ball touches any line, goes outside the court it is out of play.

  The ball is brought back into play by a non-offending player either (*a*) at a point on the end line after a basket or (*b*) at a point on the side line nearest where it went out of play.

Other Possible Additions

Three-second rule: this rule should be applied very leniently to discourage 'goal hanging' and encourage team play. Rule forbids players to be in their opponents' free throw zone for more than three seconds when their team has the ball.

Substitution: teams of 8 to 10 can be chosen, boys, girls or mixed, and players may be substituted at any time when the ball is dead.

These rules may be used as a guide towards establishing a basketball type of game within the games programme, but there is no suggestion that they must be slavishly observed. If, however, several schools wish at some time to play one another on a rally or friendly basis some agreed framework of rules is essential, otherwise different local interpretation of the rules can cause havoc. The rules suggested here would serve this purpose very well, and would also be a very firm foundation on which to base lower Secondary and where applicable Middle school basketball training and competition.

If a free-flowing game can be established in which the skills of passing, dribbling and shooting are obvious, and the emphasis is on attacking and high scoring, all that one would wish for has been achieved. The players should mark an opponent, move frequently and freely, avoid contact and above all ENJOY themselves.

Cricket

In its full sense this is probably the most complicated and costly game in the Junior school games programme. All the finer skills of batting and bowling as understood by cricketers are quite beyond the 'limit of interest' of children unused to the facilities and personal tuition necessary for their inculcation. The exceptional boy has often been quoted to disprove this statement, but in real terms of the great majority in the skills of batting and bowling they are starting from ground level, often using grass surfaces which at best are unpredictable.

Despite these difficulties the idea of playing cricket still has a great basic appeal to many boys, and presented enjoyably can become a 'life activity' for some of them. It also has a number of skills such as throwing, catching and fielding which need no alteration, merely more practice allied to the situations of this particular game. Using these skills as a base for group practices, coaching batting and bowling on class and later group lines and including adapted 'all involved all the time' small-side games of cricket would appear to be the most profitable approach especially in games lessons.

Organized along this basic pattern, usually in natural ability groups cricket can be made active, enjoyable, and worth while. If, however, the main emphasis is placed on trying to play cricket in the games lesson, many less able youngsters will fail so utterly and finally that their interest can never be revived, and they will simply become expert producers of 'daisy chains and mischief'.

Equipment

Wide price variations, recommended sizes only.

Bats: sizes 6, 5 and 4 – vellum covered or specially treated bats well worth consideration for heavy 'learner' usage.

Bat shapes, ideal for mass coaching, sizes 4, 5 and 6 available quite cheaply, using softer ball.

Balls: lacrosse, tennis, composition and particularly soft cored 'pudding' cricket ball. Cricket balls for this age-range should be $4\frac{3}{4}$ oz. – important for grip. Buy few and guard them well, otherwise their useful life will be limited.

Wickets: chalked on wall, highly recommended, cheap, always available, portable, usually allows batsman best playing surface available in school, no wicket-keeper required. Playground stumps, swivel base, very useful, 26 to 28 in. Cricket stumps – 2 sets of 26-in. usually required.

Protective clothing: essential, otherwise self preservation becomes dominant feature.

    2 pairs of wicket-keeping pads and gloves (boys size).
    4 pairs of batting pads (boys size).
    4 pairs of batting gloves (boys size).

Wearing pads and gloves should be encouraged to the point of automatic acceptance including time for padding up in all practices involving batting and wicket-keeping.

Pitches: playground often best 'learning and playing' surface, other important factors such as school windows, main roads being considered.

Grass – level and cut to reasonable length often best one can hope for.

Recommended sizes: under 11: 18 to 19 yds. Over 11 to 13: 19 to 21 yds.

Many Secondary schools have 'artificial' strips laid down on their field which require little or no maintenance, can be stored in the winter and give a relatively true surface on which to play at a moment's notice. This type of facility may become available more widely in the future, and would certainly greatly assist the encouragement of cricket in a large number of Junior schools whose field facilities nationally are far inferior to those found in Secondary schools.

The future of cricket as a major summer game at Secondary school level may very well depend on its method of presentation at top Junior and Middle school stages. It is now being challenged by a constantly widening range of activities in later school life, and if one's earliest experiences were in the 8 to 11 batting order, followed by being extra, extra long stop, it is unlikely to enter the 'choice' field when it is presented. Since many levels of cricket exist in later life this early losing of interest is particularly unfortunate, and should be avoided by deliberate lower and wider presentation at this stage.

Batting

Slow but steady progress should be the aim in acquiring this particular art, since it basically conflicts with the natural use of a club. A great deal of previous skill learning has to be modified before regular success can be achieved. Group coaching using bat shapes, hand feeding to marked areas, will ensure maximum activity and control of this difficult learning situation. If pupils leave the Junior school appreciating the value of the recommended strokes, still willing to 'hit' the ball, particularly to the side of the wicket on which it pitches, great success will have been achieved.

During adapted games which follow, a generous interpretation of the motto, 'not how but how many', with special praise for good effective shots as they occur, should be one's guide. Coach skills hard and regularly but once the 'game' starts, verbal encouragement should be the limit of interruption.

Practices: using playground or level grass, bat shapes, tennis or pudding balls.

Grip and Stance: essentially individual providing the hands are gripping the bat in the correct order, i.e. left hand uppermost for right-handers, and that they do indeed grip the bat – avoid the right index finger extension down back of bat handle. Major points of stance should be – both eyes on bowler, easy natural position from which the bat may be confidently brought into play.

Pairs: hand feeding from 3 to 4 yds hitting back to feeder many times will enable any major faults, i.e. hands in wrong order, leaning on the bat to be remedied.

Straight Bat: the 'major' difficulty – wall charts or good demonstration invaluable. Aim for the straighter bat, showing the value of straightening bat for covering the wickets (see diagram). Coach movement required without using the ball – repeat short sessions of this dummy coaching regularly, gradually emphasizing the accompanying left foot forward action.

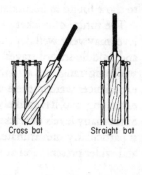

Cross bat   Straight bat

1. Threes: feed from 3 or 4 yds – play forward to bowler; extra man fields erratic returns – many turns each. The feeding is all important and must be checked.
2. Threes or fours: fed on the 'off' – hit to off side.
3. Threes or fours: fed to leg – hit to leg.
4. Fours: fed straight, off, leg – correct stroke.

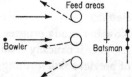

Attacking strokes such as the 'drive' have greater appeal than defensive strokes, and the above groups can be switched to straight driving, off and leg driving by altering the feed area slightly nearer to the batsman, and encouraging the batsman to take a step forward, drive and follow through.

Backward Defensive: often very difficult, should not be over-emphasized.

Using same groups move feed areas farther away from batsman who practises stepping back to cover his wicket and letting the ball hit the bat, with left elbow high. In this age-range playing such a stroke to a straight ball is often sufficient.

Having got this retreating action, use it to inculcate the idea that by taking such an action it is possible to hit balls delivered on the leg side very hard to that side. If the 'retirement to square leg' can be cured early all other disappointments are well worth while. Over and over again, using feeders and target areas, feed on this side using two fielders and three balls per group. The purity of the strokes can be emphasized later – the essential appreciation and value of the movement is all important. In game situations it is essential that the batsman wears pads and where possible gloves for this learning to become effective.

Little time is usually available for cricket, therefore together with the other skills to be acquired, and lacking net facilities it is suggested that the foregoing essentials will more than suffice at this stage. Group practices later followed by adapted games in which one mistake does not necessarily curtail an innings will enable the rudiments of quite complicated skills to be acquired as enjoyably and actively as possible.

Bowling

Some boys experience little difficulty in acquiring the essentials of over-arm bowling and grouped together in twos or fours can profitably practise particularly to improve their length. Many, however, will be starting a new and apparently very difficult skill which must be built up slowly stage by stage.

Stages:
A. Action
Sideways on to batsman, left arm high, looking over left shoulder keeping body upright and swing right arm over near the ear releasing the ball forward at top of arm swing, without the ball.

1. Pairs: action, release, catch, returned bowled by partner – 12 to 15 yds apart.
2. Pairs: add three-pace run up, i.e. right, left, right – wide base and bowl – many practices build in necessary follow through to complete basic action.

Run-up tends to be highly individual – stress, however, the need to make it short and regular – releasing ball in correct direction at steady speed.

B. *Direction*

Using wickets, wall wickets, skittles, boxes, i.e. 'objective'.

Pairs or fours: gradually increasing range to 18 to 19 yds – bowling for direction only arrange as follows:

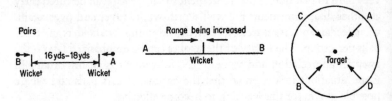

Aim: known run-up, overarm action with follow through, on or very near target.

C. *Length*

Only guided practice can achieve definite results for majority – boys made to bowl may eventually learn on 'hit or miss' principle but usually only after ruining the batsman's practice by providing him with a mixture of 'four bouncers, daisy cutters, and lobbed dolly drops'.

1. Sixes: four bowlers, wicket-keeper and ball returner as in diagram.

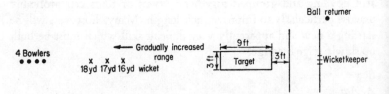

2. Later, grouping faster learners together, reduce target area – scoring both activities as 2 for ball of good length, i.e. in target, and 1 for hitting wickets – 3 for both. Personal score for 2 or 3 overs – try to beat your own score.

Spin and Speed

Although the three basic essentials of action, direction and length are quite sufficient from the teacher's point of view, there is some deep-seated desire in almost every boy to bowl fast which must be given some scope for release. The most one can often hope to do to assist is to arrange such practice with limited run-up space, to prevent high speed cross-country practice occurring.

Spinning the ball can often be included as a group practice – showing the grips and actions either personally or by wall chart, and then encouraging early practice with Sorbo rubber or tennis balls underhand in pairs. Groups of three or four using a playbat, and soft ball can be arranged on lines similar to those detailed for early batting practices. Overarm spin bowling in pairs can be introduced, preferably to those boys who have shown signs of mastering the major basic actions noting those to whom spinning the ball comes most naturally.

Batting and bowling should be brought together at the earliest time possible, using groups of six to nine, building towards single wicket, and non-stop cricket involving all cricket skills.

Catching, Throwing and Fielding

Realistically cricket of any reasonable kind must be played with a hard ball, and although early practices of these skills may be made with soft rubber and tennis balls, more solid and slightly weightier projectiles should be introduced. Soft-cored 'pudding' type cricket balls are ideal, giving a realistic 'feel' to the activity without frightening the learners. A very useful acquisition, which is relatively inexpensive, easy to store, and appealing to all ability levels is a 'slip catcher'. This piece of equipment may also be used for other games lessons involving throwing and catching such as rounders and stoolball.

Practices

1. Individual throwing and catching: in air, from bounce and particularly where possible from rebound surfaces such as walls incorporating the overarm throw and aiming spots on the wall. Concentration on the correct catching action.
2. Pairs: underarm throwing and catching using harder ball from short range – slowly increasing range, height and speed of throw.

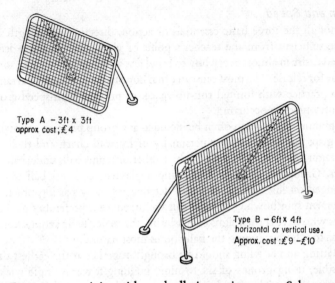

Type A – 3ft x 3ft
approx cost; £4

Type B – 6ft x 4ft
horizontal or vertical use.
Approx. cost : £9 –£10

3. Fours: same activity with gradually increasing range. Select groups carefully.
4. Pairs: overarm throwing and catching at 10 to 12 yds range – concentrating on accuracy and catching, building this up to groups of four – wicket-keeper, returner and two throwers using wickets appropriate to surface on which practice is taking place.
5. Pairs: throws landing short, fielded and returned accurately – increasing difficulty by throwing along ground to be fielded and returned to feeder standing near a single wicket.
6. Groups: target, i.e. skittle, one or two wickets, box – circular formation partners on opposite sides of circle – throwing to hit target, partner fields and throws immediately. Starting range 8 to 10 yds, pairs increase range after two or three successful hits.
7. Combined practices: increasing importance can be laid on these skills in the group coaching sessions on batting and bowling by slightly increasing these groups to include wicket-keepers and having fielders return ball EVERY time to wicket.

Games: Single wicket – groups of 10.

Ideally every boy should try his hand at batting, bowling and fielding, but such wide ability ranges are encountered particularly in bowling, a skill in which 'ability' groups are often most productive. The lower group may well still be at the underarm bowling stage and appear to have made little or no progress, but if they are actively engaged and enjoying their game together success has been achieved.

Rules

1. Each boy bats in known order for FOUR overs – scoring as many runs as he can.
2. He may only be run out at the wicket towards which he is running.
3. His total score is the difference between the runs scored and number of dismissals.
4. No L.B.W. in early stages – introduced later especially for ablest groups – must be thoroughly explained before becoming operational, i.e. did ball pitch straight or on 'off'. Would it have hit wicket?
5. Each player bowls – teacher must choose whether these are bowled consecutively or whether each batsman should experience the ploys of at least two bowlers.
6. Wicket-keeper properly clad; bats but need not bowl – very special position which needs much realistic practice.
7. Scorer may be 'walking wounded', boy predisposed to this activity or one of players who scores for half team then rotates to take full part in game.

Arrangements

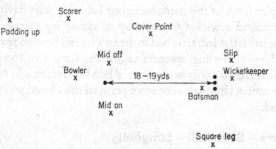

Fielders should rotate as bowler is changed, and should know the names and areas in which to operate.

These rules may be freely altered, i.e. batsmen may be given 5 or 8 minutes each, to suit conditions and personal preferences.

Non-stop Cricket: a number of variations are possible – details of one quoted involve running between wickets, tip and run rules, and great deal of fielding, catching and throwing to the wicket-keeper.

One method of play (others may be devised to emphasize different features required):

1. All batting takes place at one end, all bowling at the other end – teams 11 a side.
2. Batsman must run when he hits the ball – all dismissals at wicket-keeper's wicket.
3. Bowling may be underarm or overarm – 10 balls in an over.
4. Bowler may bowl whether batsman is ready or is out of position and if throwing is good, before next batsman is ready to play.
5. Only fully completed runs count.
6. Dismissal occurs by being bowled, caught, run-out or obstructing fielders.
7. Only pause between innings.

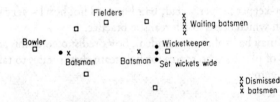

A simpler form of this game using one batsman, who having hit the ball runs round a wicket 6 yds away to square leg carrying his bat, whilst the ball is fielded, returned to the bowler and bowled again is often successful, even bowling 'spinners' underhand from 8 to 10 yds. In this game a batsman may only be dismissed if he is bowled, caught or for flagrant obstruction, although once again personal rules based on experience are advised.

Rounders – Stoolball – Longball

This group of small ball, single hitter games depend on the same skills of throwing, catching, fielding, underarm bowling, and hitting with the type of bat deemed appropriate to the game. Many children expect to play these games (especially rounders) and in many cases they already know the major rules and just want to get on with the game. If this happens to be the case the teacher has a ready made starting-point, since by watching the players in action one can observe which particular skills need developing. If in fact stoolball or longball are new games to the children, observation of their rounders ability still serves as a guide for skill development in future lessons.

These 'situation' games develop rather slowly so it is important to devise lessons related to the full game, but during which by pair or group practices all have a chance to bowl, field, throw and hit the ball. It may be necessary to use wider bats and bigger or softer balls for some groups so that some success can be achieved. Unless simple skills and practices are used before most games commence a number of children may never hit or touch the ball during the whole period.

Apparatus

Balls: tennis or Sorbo rubber balls may be used for all three games. Webbro-Lastic rounders ball and stoolball are designed to be kinder to the hands, 7s 4d.

Sticks: 5s each or preferably wider faced bats 6s to 7s each. Many play-bats especially those with built-up handles are most suitable using tennis or Sorbo balls.

Posts: multi-purpose posts with bases are ideal for both playground and field use if available. Plastic covered, steel shod posts are useful for all these games and for making portable posts for postball, soccer, rugby and are available at approximately £2 per set (4). Wide variety of objects may be used, e.g. cricket stumps, boxes, individual P.E. mats – acid test being whether the bases are easily visible.

Skills, Techniques and Practices

1. Catching: using softer balls in the early stages, deliberate coaching of following: watch ball into the hands – reach out to meet the ball with hands 'cupped' – relax arms to throwing side of body on re-ception to allay impact and to be in throwing position.
2. Throwing: underarm and overarm throws are both useful, most coaching, however, will need to be concentrated on the latter throw. It is often possible and profitable to get a 'natural thrower' to demon-strate, drawing attention to the sideways position, long slinging

arm action and the shifting of weight from rear to front culminating in good follow-through.

3. Fielding: stressing the prime need of 'anticipating path and speed of ball' so that you are able to get in direct line with ball, show crouched, knees apart, hands cupped fielding position. Later emergency pick-ups and combinations of fielding and throwing can be introduced.

4. Bowling: limiting preparatory steps to 2 or 3, and concentrating on accuracy by providing targets, all should have the opportunity of practising. These practices can usefully be allied with catching and batting – increasing speed and variety as skill develops.

5. Batting: use any bat with which they can HIT the ball regularly during practice. See grip is correct, i.e. left hand lowest when bat is raised, watch ball and hit firmly and deliberately pointing out the benefits of trying to hit the ball between or over fielders.

Practices: these skills are so dependant one upon another that many combined practices, e.g. throwing and catching, batting and fielding naturally occur. Many individual variations to suit all needs are possible therefore the practices suggested may be regarded as a basic outline of ideas on which to build a personal practice system.

1. Catching: individually, throwing upwards and catching, concentrating on catching action gradually increasing height.

2. Pairs: underarm throwing and catching gradually increasing distance, later adding 'pick-up' and throw, aiming to get ball directly to partner at waist height.

3. Groups: 4 or 5 in group circle underarm throwing and catching in all directions – everyone on the alert.

4. Pairs: overarm throwing and catching at short range concentrating on throwing action and accuracy, sometimes increasing difficulty by adding one-handed catching limitation.

5. Pairs: overarm throwing for height and catching.

6. Pairs: overarm throwing and catching gradually increasing range of throw, and aiming to make catch and return throw a continuous action.

7. Pairs: any type of throw landing short – fielded on bounce and returned immediately.

8. Groups: 6 or 8 in circular formation with post approximately 4 ft high, firmly placed in centre of circle. Throw aiming to hit post, partner either catches or fields throw and immediately attempts to hit post. The distance from the post should be increased from time to time and successes in specified time counted.

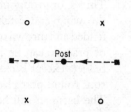

9. Pairs: rolling, fielding, throwing and catching – great variety of speeds and direction of roll can gradually be built up, partners changing function regularly.

10. Pairs: bowling and catching concentrating on bowling, i.e. two or three steps, arm swing and release trying to get the same action every time.

   (*a*) targets marked on wall – partner gets rebound

   (*b*) open targets (see diagram) – very useful since backstop practice can be added, and by making group three first base throw can complete triangle, changing after eight bowls

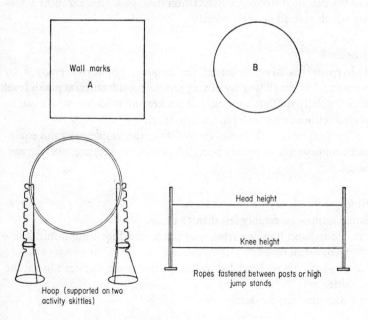

Wall marks
A

B

Hoop (supported on two activity skittles)

Head height

Knee height

Ropes fastened between posts or high jump stands

11. Threes, or groups of 4 or 5: combining batting, bowling, fielding, throwing and catching. Originally simply six balls mostly hit, fielded and thrown to bowler – all rotating. Gradually this fuller type of practice can be built into the simple type of game where all fielders except backstop must throw and catch ball while batsman runs round post placed where first base will eventually be placed. The batsman still has his six or eight bowls but finishing with a double score, i.e. three runs, two dismissals. Other simple rules may be added or subtracted as long as the game gives everybody an opportunity to hit, to bowl, to throw and to catch.

Other items of importance in the full game such as backing up the fielder, fielding and batting positions can be introduced when required. One danger to be avoided is the discarded bat – have sufficient for the runner to carry the bat to touch the posts.

Rounders

The rules and pitch markings for rounders are widely known. Many Primary School Games Associations provide copies to their members, and the National Rounders Association have produced excellent booklets which give all necessary details.

Stoolball

This game has never achieved the national popularity enjoyed by rounders, but is well worthy of very serious consideration at junior level since basically it offers a mixture of cricket and rounders which can be played without extensive pitch preparation.

Comprehensive rule books are available, the simple rules and equipment suggested here merely being adaptations in keeping with the age-range.

Rules

Equal teams – preferably less than 11 a side.
1. Underhand bowling from mid pitch, rear foot behind mid line – 6- to 8-ball overs.
2. No ball – above head, below knee, out of reach – scores 1 to batting side.
3. Batsmen may be out:

Types of bat that may be used.

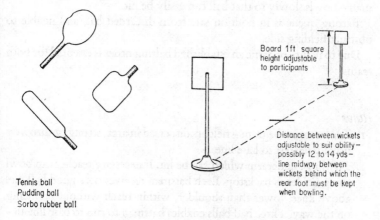

Board 1ft square
height adjustable
to participants

Distance between wickets
adjustable to suit ability –
possibly 12 to 14 yds –
line midway between
wickets behind which the
rear foot must be kept
when bowling.

Tennis ball
Pudding ball
Sorbo rubber ball

(a) bowled, i.e. ball hits face of wicket not upright
(b) caught – either full catch or if prefer after one bounce
(c) run out – ball thrown by fielder to hit wicket face, before batsman
      can touch face with bat or hand
4. Any batsman scoring 15 runs shall retire.
5. Each player bowls in turn.
6. When final two players are batting dismissal of either ends the
   innings.

Long Ball

Using tennis or hollow rubber ball, strong playbat and four markers such
as skittles, wickets, etc., as shown in diagram this game can soon be
arranged outdoors, and using large playball and the head or hand can
be played indoors where space permits, i.e. hall.

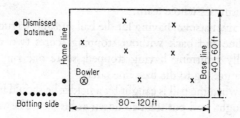

Using posts – lines unnecessary. Bowler about 10 to 15 ft from batsman – bowls slowly so that ball can easily be hit.

Batting queue is in position safe from discarded bat, and unable to
obstruct fielding side.

Due to nature of game an established batting order is essential for both
teams.

Rules

1. Teams: as in diagram – fielders dispersed in area, strongest throwers
   usually nearest to base line.
2. Bowling: underarm which can be hit. If necessary teacher can bowl
   using fielder as backstop. Each batsman receives ONE good ball, i.e.
   above knee, lower than shoulder, within reach without bouncing
   on the way. Three bad balls enables batsman to run to base line unhindered.
3. Ball may only be hit within the area defined by posts or wickets.
   Any balls hit when landing outside area, batsman dismissed.
4. After hitting the ball the batsman runs and dodges through fielders,
   who having fielded ball try to throw it to hit batsman, never taking
   more than three paces with the ball. Fielders should be encouraged
   to throw the ball to other fielders better placed than themselves
   preferably ahead of the runner and to back up all throws. If the
   batsman is hit he retires, if he reaches the base line without being
   hit he may stay there if he wishes, returning at any future time when
   the ball is in play, i.e. when the ball has been hit. Any number of
   batsmen may be at base line at same time.
5. Batsmen may be dismissed by:
   (a) hitting ball outside area
   (b) if hit by thrown ball
   (c) running outside defined area in either direction – three batsmen
       out dismisses whole team.
6. Scoring: any batsman having hit the ball and able to run and dodge
   to base line and back without stopping scores two runs. Those
   successfully returning having stopped, score one run. No run is
   scored for getting to the base line safely.
7. Caught: when the ball is caught by a fielder he should immediately
   shout 'caught' and put the ball down at his feet. The whole of the

fielding side immediately run over the home line. The batting side run out and pick up the ball and if they can by passing and throwing hit one of the fielding side BEFORE he crosses the home line they immediately resume their innings. This rule adds a great deal of enjoyment to the game but if it appears a little complicated a catch can count as a normal dismissal especially in the early stages. This is often the best rule indoors where catches may be dispensed with entirely due to restricted hitting area.

Points to be Noted

1. Fielders should be encouraged to concentrate on 'returning' runners since these are the scorers.
2. Discourage shots at outgoing runner towards base line since if they miss the runner is able to score two runs while the ball is being recovered.
3. Batsmen should be encouraged to accumulate at the base line coming back *en masse* when a suitable opportunity presents itself, since the confusion created by having so many targets often prevents the fielding side hitting any of them.
4. Number of dismissals which end an innings – personal choice.
5. Certain modifications are necessary when played indoors.

Net Games

Adapted forms of tennis and badminton are now possible within the Junior school games programme in the shape of padder tennis and batinton. The initial equipment cost and versatility of the latter makes it particularly attractive, but both can be provided very cheaply on the 'do-it-yourself' basis.

These games have a tremendous appeal and with a little coaching excellent standards of play and enjoyment can be achieved. In some areas friendly inter school rallies have already been established with great success, and when one school plays its neighbour, enormous numbers can be fully employed both physically and vocally.

Padder Tennis

Apparatus: complete sets for four, prices range from £8 to £15 depending on design and quality. By making stands and posts (see diagram), and buying bats and net this can be reduced to £3 to £4, enabling greater numbers to be equipped.

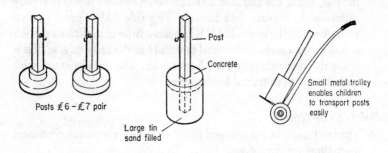

Post

Concrete

Posts £6 – £7 pair

Small metal trolley enables children to transport posts easily

Large tin sand filled

Court: lines 1½ in. wide – best permanently marked on playground.

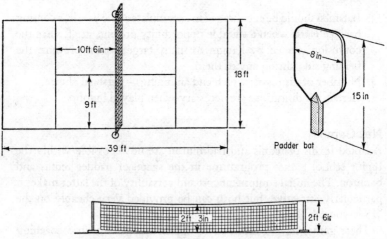

←10ft 6in→

18 ft

9 ft

39 ft

8 in

15 in

Padder bat

2ft 3in

2ft 6in

Net height

Rules

Numbers: singles or doubles, same court dimensions used.

Service: first service in each game from right into alternate court – feet behind base line – two attempts may be made.

Singles: players serve alternately, i.e. when you serve you can score or lose serve.

Doubles: A and B *v*. C and D – A serves first, C second, B third and D fourth. Service may be underarm or overarm – once correctly in play the ball may be hit on the volley or before it hits ground twice. Line ball is IN.

Scoring: first point: 15; second point: 30; third point: 40; fourth point: game; ties on fourth point: deuce; two clear points then decides game. A player who first wins six games wins a set, except that he must win by a margin of at least two games. Three sets shall decide a match.

Within schools other systems of scoring may be adopted – the one above is recommended.

Practices
Using padder or large playbats and tennis or hollow rubber balls outdoors, and gamester balls indoors.

Individual
1. Hitting up: allow to bounce once – hit again, using alternate bat faces.
2. Hitting up: keep it up – using either bat face.
3. Line painted on wall 2 ft 6 in. from ground – deliberate forehand stroke practice – early stages concentration on contact, gradually building up to greater range, variety of angles and speed and including volley return.
4. Same practice limited to backhand strokes only.
5. Progress to continuous practice of this activity involving both forehand and backhand strokes.
6. Excellent practice of this kind can be obtained if a 'corner' is used – at a later stage pairs can use such a space to practise by playing a simple game involving alternate hits on volley or rebound above line, server only scoring.
7. Serving practice can also be practised – line 19 ft 6 in. away on floor – one versus one game, or even doubles can be introduced as group activity.

Pairs
1. Hitting up, bounce, partner hits up, short range, continuous hits. Count hits.

2. Partner feeds by hand – forehand stroke – catch by partner who feeds again. This can be built into quite advanced practice by varying pace and direction of feed and having partner move obliging stroke player still send catch at waist height to partner.

3. Partner feeds by hand – backhand strokes – built up in the same way as number 2.

4. Partner feeds either side – appropriate stroke resulting. Some difficulty may be experienced in training 'correct feeding', but it is well worth persevering since deliberate controlled practice is only possible in this way.

5. Partner feeds to stroke maker who is standing near net – necessity of controlled downward smash can be stressed. It is useful to use groups of three for this practice: one hitter, one feeder with three or four balls and a retriever – group rotating functions.

6. Pairs on either side of net or rope – STRESS CO-OPERATION in early stages – link these practices directly with numbers 2, 3 and 4, i.e. hand feed forehand stroke and follow by repeating practice across net or rope, each player now with bat. Count successful hits. If this is done in a competitive manner from the beginning, learning will suffer as the skill constantly breaks down resulting in mounting frustration as the ball is being constantly chased.

7. Service can be introduced into these pair practices. If necessary allow early serves to be taken nearer net, gradually working back to base line.

Positions for doubles play can be explained indoors, at the same time explaining scoring system. Given the opportunity children are quite capable of becoming very efficient umpires, line judges and scorers especially for games periods and inter-class rallies.

Games Lessons

Each lesson should end with an opportunity to 'have a go', and since full courts may be limited in number the following arrangement is one possible way of presenting the game and allied activities.

Groups rotate – pass two places per week.

Batinton

Basically batinton is scaled-down badminton using table tennis scoring. Being extremely adaptable for a number of net games and relatively in-

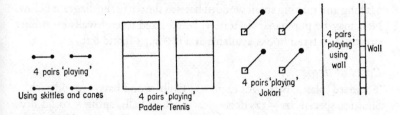

4 pairs 'playing'
Using skittles and canes

4 pairs 'playing'
Padder Tennis

4 pairs 'playing'
Jokari

4 pairs 'playing' using wall

Wall

expensive this is an excellent 'buy', particularly for Junior schools which have a hall. The initial cost can easily be reduced by a little 'do-it-your-self', giving apparatus with which it is possible to play batinton with shuttle or small gamester ball, indoor padder tennis, quoit tennis, batinton volley and volleyball for juniors.

Apparatus

Complete set for four including posts, net, shuttles, gamester ball and plastic handled cork-faced bats – £4. Same equipment with wooden bats – £3 10s.

Guys and pegs are also included making it possible to erect the appara-tus out-of-doors.

Do it yourself

Using high jump stands, multi-purpose posts with extra wooden tops bringing them to 5 ft, or preferably purchasing a number of sturdy posts

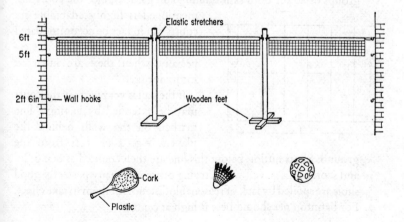

Elastic stretchers

6ft
5ft

2ft 6in — Wall hooks   Wooden feet

Cork
Plastic

6 ft long and making small wooden bases as shown in the diagram below. Nets may be purchased separately, being fixed to end walls by rubber stretchers to fixed hooks available at 2 ft 6 in., 5 ft and 6 ft.

Costs of Items

'Standard' plastic bats – 12s each.   'Club' wood bats – 10s 6d each.
Shuttles, special size – 12s doz.   Airflow balls, sprite – 9s 6d doz.

Existing playbats and gamester balls may be used, but purchase of the special rubber nosed small size plastic shuttle is desirable especially to get the game off to a good start.

Rules (using table tennis scoring method – badminton scoring method or indeed any other which works well may be used if preferred):

  1. Court:

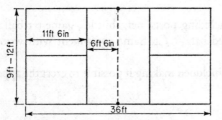

Juniors are quite happy to play without line markings – if lines are to be marked, lines between adjoining courts are preferred.

Junior school hall marked for six games of batinton, using essential markings only (as in diagram) could profitably be used for groups of 40 for both skill training and games. Since the court size mentioned is highly adaptable six courts can in fact be accommodated in much smaller halls than this especially when they are intended for junior use.

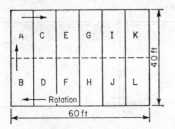

If the hall is very narrow the court may be extended by having a line marked on the walls behind the players, e.g. 4 or 5 ft from the ground. Shots hitting below this line are then counted as being 'in' and score. This is well worth trying otherwise many perfectly good shots are spoiled by lack of reasonable distance for them to take effect.

  2. For batinton net should be 5 ft high at centre.

3. Service: underhand, starting from right-hand service court into diagonal receiver's court – only one service in each court.
4. Faults: shuttle falling outside lines, into or under net, hit on opponent's side of the net.
5. Scoring (table tennis style): singles A *v.* B. A serves 5 times from alternate courts. Points won to A, points lost to B, e.g. A3, B2; B then serves 5 times, etc. Doubles A and B *v.* C and D. A serves 5 times, then C, followed in turn by B and D.

If both sides have scored 20 points, play continues with alternate service until one side has a clear lead of 2 points.

Introducing the Game

1. In pairs or small groups of four hitting the shuttle as many times as possible.
2. Same activity over the net, without limiting number of hits before return – CO-OPERATION.
3. Practise the serve, combining it with last activity – once established let them play either explaining scoring system referred to previously or one of own invention.
4. Early play may well be rather hurried and in some cases rather desperate also – the game is not quite so simple as it appears, and frequent breaks in play to pick up the shuttle will occur. It is important therefore to work on simple skills before each new session of play, e.g.:
5. Pairs: each 3 ft from net – hitting and returning gradually moving farther away from net without breaking rhythm – try to encourage the high 'clear' to rear of court.
6. Pairs: starting at rear of court – hitting and returning gradually moving closer to the net using both forehand and backhand strokes as appropriate – encourage 'drop' shot.
7. Pairs: feeder 6 ft from net putting up high shots for partner to run in and 'smash'. Emphasize the necessity of hitting the shuttle on one's own side of the net without touching the net – otherwise this fault will occur frequently in later play.

Later Stages

1. *Service Strokes*

Different types of service can be shown and practised **viz:**

(a) short, low service – just skim-
ming over the net with little
power, forcing an upward
return

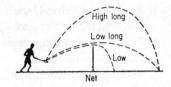

(b) high, long service – used when
opponent is too far forward,
forcing him to run back to return the shuttle hurriedly

(c) low, long service – only for occasional use as a surprise stroke

(d) differing angles at which it is possible to serve can later be introduced

2. Receiving Service

When returning service and in play generally there are four main shots
used:

(a) 'Clear', i.e. high drive to back
of opponent's court – height
is all important otherwise it
can be 'smashed'.

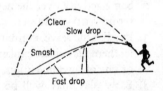

(b) 'Slow drop': should be used
interspersed with other shots
to take opponent by surprise.

(c) 'Smash': stress wristy downward action necessary to produce
winners.

(d) 'Fast drop': shuttle hit hard to skim across top of net to mid-
court – often preferable to smash.

3. Positions of Partners

At first players tend to stand as a pair on the mid-line of the court. The
idea of server or receiver playing near net with partner covering the back
of the court can be introduced gradually to great advantage. Try to
encourage players to play the shuttle as early as possible and preferably
above net height.

4. Umpiring

Children can become excellent umpires over a period of time. They
should be encouraged to give clear decisions and to be in charge of their
particular court. Umpiring leads to greater understanding of the game
and as many as possible should be given the chance to be 'in charge' from
time to time.

Possible Class or Rally Organization

Using six courts as shown in previous diagram – twelve teams of three can be chosen.

Team A *v*. team B on court 1 – extra A to be umpire, extra B to be scorer. Team C *v*. team D on court 2 using extra players to umpire and score.

Games may either be decided on three sets, or since time is often pressing on leaders on each court after determined time, e.g. 10 minutes.

Rotation then takes place by all teams moving one court to left – except those teams which have wall to their left who simply move forward to the other side of the court on which they have just played. When facing new opponents one of the previous players in each three becomes the 'extra' man and takes on umpiring or scoring duties. Since possibly only two or three changes per session will be possible a record of where to start next time must be kept so that finally every group has played every other group.

Variations using same Equipment

Batinton Volley: using the gamester ball and a net height of 5 ft, this variation can be introduced quite simply by altering the service to the rear line of the court. The ball can then be returned on the volley or after it has bounced once. Juniors find this game somewhat difficult due to the speed of the ball on a small court and two or three bounces sometimes help the game in the early stages.

Padder Tennis: reducing the net height to 2 ft 6 in. enables the rules of padder previously described to be applied – preferably starting with an underhand serve from base line.

Quoit Tennis: net at 5 ft – quoit served from base line and returned by receiver lower than shoulder height. The quoit must be cleanly caught in one hand and returned by alternate players until a fault occurs – use batinton scoring.

Junior Volleyball: net height 6 ft, light size 4 or 5 Frido, teams of four to six. Starting by throwing and catching across the net, each team touching ball three times before returning, build up to volleying ball with both hands. Simple underhand hit to serve then 'volleying' back and forward, trying to encourage more than one volley between team-mates before returning. Batinton scoring may be used – team taking turns to serve.

Athletics

Many areas have very well organized and enjoyable Sports Days which have become part of the 'sporting calendar'. The events offered at this meeting, however, have a marked tendency to feedback and determine the athletic programme of the individual schools concerned. There is much in athletics at its root sources of running, jumping and throwing which can be adapted to provide enjoyable, and mildly competitive activity for the majority of children of this age. Junior schools should place their main emphasis on arranging their own 'Sports Day', planning their programme to accommodate the maximum numbers in enjoyable competition well within a normal school afternoon. Since on such occasions the school is on public display the meeting must be efficiently arranged and managed without detracting from the competitors' or spectators' enjoyment.

Preliminary Considerations

To assist planning.

1. Examination of facilities and equipment – assuming agreed 'all-involved' policy.
2. Consideration of events, i.e. short sprints increasing distance with age, simple throws, e.g. cricket ball, rounders ball, football, possibly to be decided before sports day, jumps – long and high, forms of obstacle race, i.e. potato, egg and spoon, sack, hurdles and finally some form of team relays.
3. Training for events – it may be decided to have a self competitive simple 'standards' system using a compiled set of standards, or preferably setting two or three targets within the school. This system has much to recommend it, and with individual cards can be operated by the children, encouraging practise against oneself in a wide variety of activities.

   Examples of standards – these standards were published in 1931 by the Ling Conference and are partially quoted here to provide a starting guide, excellent copies of the most recent tables are available from Southern Counties AAA, 26 Park Crescent, London W1.

Event	Boys (age)				Girls (age)			
	8	9	10	11	8	9	10	11
	ft in	ft in	ft in	ft in	ft in	ft in	ft in	ft in
St Broad Jump	3 4	3 8	4 0	4 6	3 0	3 4	3 8	4 1
Long Jump	6 0	6 6	7 0	8 3	5 6	5 9	6 0	6 3
High Jump	2 2	2 5	2 8	2 11	2 0	2 2	2 6	2 9
Football Throw	14 0	16 0	18 0	20 0	12 0	14 0	16 0	18 0
Football Sling	19 0	22 0	26 0	29 0	13 0	15 0	17 0	19 0
Cricket ball			25 yd	30 yd				
	sec	sec	sec	sec	sec	sec	sec	sec
30 yards	6·1	6·0	5·4	5·3	6·3	6·3	6.2	6·0
40 yards	7·4	7·3	7·2	7·1	8·2	8·1	8·0	7·3
50 yards	9·0	8·4	8·3	8·2	9·3	9·2	9·1	9·0
60 yards	—	11·2	10·4	10·3	—	—	—	—
75 yards	—	—	—	12·3	—	—	—	—
100 yards	—	—	—	15·2	—	—	—	—

Short sprints are often very difficult to operate under this system but many other activities such as jumps and throws of many kinds can profitably be encouraged in this way. Having a high and low standard in each event enables every child to contribute to the unit on which it is decided to operate. If this UNIT can be reduced from house to class level, and entry limited to one or two events and the relay or relay game almost full involvement is assured. The standards must be included in the overall scoring and progress in this preliminary field should be posted as a running total before the sports.

4. Fix date, with alternative – decide on staff allocation for duties as stewards, judges, starter, recorders and pen supervisors using local contacts of retired staff, and interested parents who are often invaluable on such occasions.

5. Contact L.E.A. where such facilities exist to have necessary markings put down well in advance so that they may be used for practice, and re-marked for the great day. If such assistance is not available use local contacts and if necessary as is often the case take your coat off and set to work with able children assisting.

Nearly all Junior school teachers are at some time involved in assisting at the school sports in some capacity. Essential duties such as pen supervision or stewarding competitors to the start are part of the teacher's working life. Recording is straightforward given the necessary forms by the teacher in charge, but it would appear that some guidance on starting and judging would be helpful to many teachers.

Starting:

Using 'voice', clapper board, starting pistol – whistle for recall. Normally one deals with large numbers delivered to the all important line.

1. Ensure they are prepared to judge the finish.
2. Stand where you can see all competitors.
3. Calm, friendly approach even in moments of dire stress.
4. Your job is to see 'fair play', i.e. nothing over line before 'GO'.
5. Simple regular words of command – suggest 'Get set' – 'GO'. If there is any doubt in your mind about the fairness of the start, blow whistle and recall runners

Judging:

Due to large numbers involved over such short distances a tape fixed at chest height per age-range is most useful.

1. Stand in line with finishing posts.
2. Concentrate on judging 1, 2 and 3 'chests' across the line.
3. Consult with other judges – establish order – give it clearly to chief judge who fills in results slip which is sent immediately to recorder.
4. Return to your place and when all is ready, signal starter that you are prepared for next race. An alternative system sometimes used is to have place cards which are given to the winning competitors who take them to the recorder.

Judging:

Long Jump: Before starting see that the PIT IS DUG, there is a rake available, and that you have three assistants, namely a raker and two tape operators. DO NOT USE PEGS.

1. Stand watching take-off area – recording board at the ready. Child holding measuring end of tape next to you, other child holds zero end of tape.
2. Call jumper, judge if no-jump, i.e. any part over edge of board.
3. Good jump – zero placed on nearest mark made to take off, tape stretched to take-off line, distance recorded whilst sand is raked.

4. After three jumps each – score best attempt of each jumper and place in order.

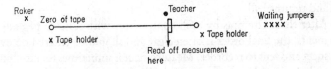

Avoid innumerable jumps into increasing sand hole and pegging distance jumped – the job cannot be 'fairly' done in this way. It is just as speedy and efficient to do it as suggested here, acquiring your help-mates by any means you choose. For your own peace of mind keep the run-up area clear, otherwise life becomes more and more difficult.

High Jump: PIT MUST BE DUG. If mats are being used, see that they are secure. Acquire four assistants, two to operate bar, rope or lath, one to operate the measuring rod which is useful even when stands are marked and the inevitable raker where needed.

1. Allow practice within reason over low bar.
2. Establish jumping order, see bar set at decided height, and make sure competitors know the rules under which the competition is being held, i.e. two or three consecutive failures eliminate.
3. Record each attempt – advising those eliminated of their demise in kindly manner.
4. Try to establish starting height realistically to avoid protracting the event.
5. Be prepared to accept ties even for first place.
6. See equipment is taken to store.

Judging Throwing: SAFETY all important, keep spectators well away, and institute unvarying system of projectile return, i.e. rolled or carried, NEVER thrown back.

1. See throwing area is clearly marked (a line will suffice), and make sure all children know that stepping over the line whilst throwing makes that throw a no-throw for judging.
2. Marking judge should have numbered or named pegs, i.e. cricket stumps serve well, and at least one ball returner and assistant spotter to help establish reasonable 'flow' of the event.
3. Judge 1 attends to throwing end recording throws, noting no-throws

and most important making sure that throws are taken in the correct order and at correct time, i.e. when field judge is ready.

Judge 2 spots and marks all good throws, whilst his assistant fields and returns ball.

4. After three attempts by each competitor, with suitable peg adjustments, the final order is often clear and should be entered on event sheet and sent to recorder. Measurement is sometimes required and is really advisable in any case. This should be done as in long jump – zero to point of impact, readings taken and noted where tape cuts the throwing line.

In view of time element most jumping and throwing events are usually decided before Sports Day, an arrangement which often helps concentrate both children and spectators within given areas. Other 'standard' events which might precede the great day such as standing broad jump, standing triple jump, running hops, soccer throw-ins for distance, shuttle runs, can be permanently marked on the playground available for practice at any time. These are well worth consideration since they can be used for group activities in the weeks preceeding the sports especially to good effect.

The majority of Junior schools have established their chosen events on the basis of years of experience and the mixture of sprints, hurdles and obstacle races of various types normally encountered is admirably suited to the children's interests. Some difficulty and uneasiness arises when the final relays come to be considered especially when all previous events have been along straight lanes. One solution which has much to recommend it is to end with some form of team shuttle relay, preferably without batons. Some ideas along these lines would be as follows:

Using two lanes per team – single runner – distance adjustable to age – teams four to eight.

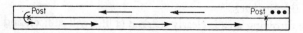

Using two lanes per team – complete shuttle – change on touch, return to original place at finish, i.e. two trips each runner.

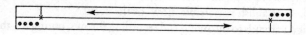

Using two lanes per team – shuttle with swerve – change on touch – once again race can end either once or twice through.

This type of relay is easier to arrange, has immediate appeal, and can be staged in front of spectators (child and adult), and can involve larger teams. Its greatest difficulty is controlling the exchanges, a problem which can be solved by introducing a baton which may be dropped without disqualification, or by the use of new shuttle relay equipment now available which, operated in two lanes as suggested, guarantees complete equity no matter how excited the competitors become. The method of operation is shown in the diagram, the equipment being available from the makers of Cantabrian Athletic Equipment.

Using this type of relay as the final event of the sports, a plan of the field arrangements for the whole sports might appear as below:

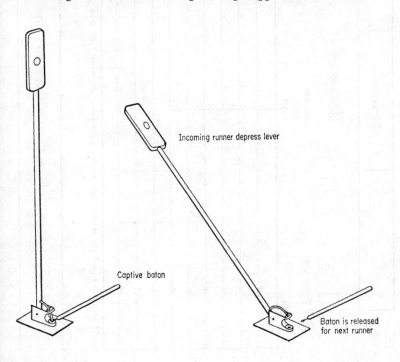

Incoming runner depress lever

Captive baton

Baton is released for next runner

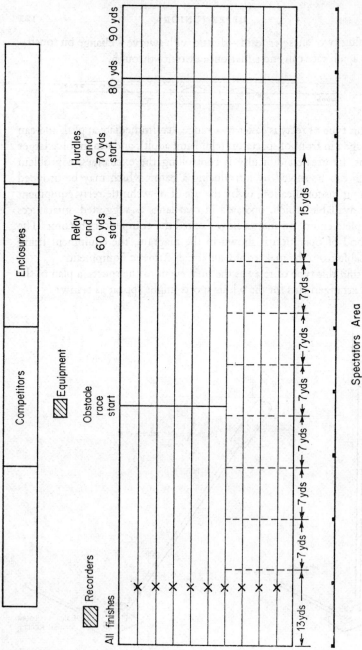

This plan envisages the inclusion of the following events with the minimum of 'furniture' removal during the course of the sports.

1. Sprints of 90, 80, 70 and 60 yds according to age on 'creeping' start basis.
2. 70 yds hurdles – hurdles in position – removed to accommodate relay game at end.
3. Short start near equipment storage for obstacle races, e.g. sack, egg and spoon, etc.
4. Unobstructed view for children and spectators.
5. Five double lanes for relay or relay game – placing turning posts either on the finishing line or 10 yds in as shown here, and arranging teams so that the last runner crosses the finishing line, i.e. odd numbers in team if shuttling.

Many amendments can be made to the programme according to personal preference, but clear planning along simple lines will greatly assist all concerned. Any attempts to introduce adult events and attitudes to athletics should be resisted, otherwise the whole 'feeling' of these unique meetings will be lost.

Lower Secondary – Middle School Stage

The range of events taught will gradually increase with increasing age and ability presenting an opportunity of success range unique within one activity. Use of standard individual record cards, potted sports, inter-form meetings, and inter-group cumulative scoring, field event competitions involving as many as possible would be well worth consideration. Some youngsters have a natural inclination to assist by judging, equipment supervision, listing arrangements, which give them a feeling of being connected with the activity in hand. In the type of programme envisaged for this age-range such assistance with a little guidance becomes tremendously beneficial for both teacher and taught, and should be given every encouragement.

The success achieved must be judged on the interest and enthusiasm created, and not solely on the trophy and badge count achieved usually by the early maturers.

Chapter 6: Middle Schools

Middle Schools

Areas in which Middle schools have been, or are about to be set up will have the opportunity to establish a games programme based on the all important years previously split between Upper Juniors and Lower Secondary levels. Although problems such as staffing, facilities and time-tabling will obviously be encountered, they should only be seriously considered after the major decisions on policy have been settled.

In the area of games there would appear to be at least three major approaches to be investigated for an age-range of 9 to 13. The first would be to have the formal major games approach usual at Lower Secondary level filtering downwards, determining the programme for the nines to elevens. The opposite flow, i.e. more informal, less competitive approach Upper Juniors influencing the whole programme would naturally then follow for consideration; and finally a double system based on the different emphasis for each age-range as set out in the present study.

There can be little doubt that if the Lower Secondary emphasis be-comes the adopted policy it will be a disaster for the majority of the younger children who will be placed in an environment which ignores their physical and mental stage of development. Younger children aspire to the standards established for the 'top' of the school, and under this emphasis it is not difficult to imagine the type of programme which would gradually evolve.

The double system would appear attractive, setting up two systems linked by a magic bridge which children crossed half-way through their stay in the school. If, however, education is to be truly regarded as a continuing and continuous process this type of policy would appear to be basically unsound, and loaded with problems for the establishment of school unity. Realistically, however, the difficulties of resisting these ready-made and established patterns of games will be considerable from a variety of sources within and without the school, and some schools may adopt them just to get started. Once this happens the cause is almost lost, since despite the difficulties it is much easier to start a new approach aligned with the other approaches in the school at the beginning rather than to change horses later.

Major upheavals in the world of physical education have occurred by junior work filtering upwards, particularly in gymnastics whose whole emphasis has been radically changed from below. Middle schools have the chance to influence greatly our whole approach to the teaching of games and games skills. Using a mixture of specialist and general teachers they can approach this area of the child's education without a ready-made fixture list to condition their every movement. Competitive fixtures can be arranged slowly over a number of years in a wide variety of ways, i.e. inter-class, inter-group, friendlies, rallies. There is no inherent evil in competition, and games must have an aim particularly for the able children who must not be forgotten in the mad rush to do our best for every child. If competitions become over fierce, and cause bad feelings between staff and schools, there is no difficulty in 'quitting the field' and establishing other levels of play more in accord with the educational needs of the children.

The policy of continuing the approaches recommended here through the school would possibly be difficult to implement during the first two years of the school's life mainly due to the experiences at a previous school of the new top forms. Once this period has passed, a continuously developing games programme could be established aligned to the overall educational policy of the school, which would greatly benefit many children usually discarded and discounted in the games sense by this stage. The activities for Upper Juniors would be developed at skill and tactical levels over a wide range of activities, retaining as one's principal guide the creation of planned, purposeful enjoyable activity. Teachers working in this field will have the opportunity to create a new attitude towards participation in games and physical activity including early training in changing and showering which could have widespread effects. We are approaching the age of leisure, which will create problems of enormous magnitude unless some positive steps towards preparing today's children for this eventuality are taken. Physical activity has a part to play in a variety of ways at many ages in the use of free time, and if this early opportunity can be used to train children in a selection of skills for immediate and later use, and most important, create an 'enjoyable memory' and favourable attitude, it will have been most profitably used.

Subject Index